Navigating Work and Life Boundaries

"An extremely timely and valuable contribution to help address big challenges facing managers and employees during and after the pandemic - how to address the increasing blurring of our work and personal lives, with the attendant costs to wellness and effectiveness. As technology permeates all aspects of our lives it is incumbent upon us to address the unintended effects. This work provides a very well-researched diagnosis of the issues and clear recommendations for managers who want to address the work/life balance challenges of their teams, especially as related to knowledge work. The focus on globally distributed collaboration, with the heightened time zone, communication and culture challenges is unique and particularly helpful."

—Dan Elron, *Managing Director, Strategy, Innovation and Technology, Accenture*

Saonee Sarker · Manju Ahuja ·
Suprateek Sarker · Kirsten M. Bullock

Navigating Work and Life Boundaries

Insights for Distributed Knowledge Professionals

palgrave
macmillan

Saonee Sarker
Lund University
Lund, Sweden

Manju Ahuja
University of Louisville
Louisville, KY, USA

Suprateek Sarker
University of Virginia
Charlottesville, VA, USA

Kirsten M. Bullock
University of Louisville
New Albany, IN, USA

ISBN 978-3-030-72758-1 ISBN 978-3-030-72759-8 (eBook)
https://doi.org/10.1007/978-3-030-72759-8

This Palgrave Macmillan imprint is published by the registered company Springer Nature Switzerland AG
The registered company address is: Gewerbestrasse 11, 6330 Cham, Switzerland

Dedicated to my parents, Late Jyotirmoy Roy and Late Sudeshna Roy, whose memory continues to inspire me each day
—Saonee Sarker

To my daughter, Nikita, who, by her mere existence, inspired me to seek a balanced work-life
—Manju Ahuja

Dedicated to my parents, Late Bhabani Prosad Sarker and Sunanda Sarker, whose love and values have made me who I am today
—Suprateek Sarker

Acknowledgments

The authors gratefully acknowledge the contributions and/or encouragement of Xiao Xiao, Steve Marlar, Debasish Jana, Jan Ondrus, Shafer Brown, Suranjan Chakraborty, Julia Kotlarsky, Ilan Oshri, Jay Mookherje, Chandrachur Sarker, Sanjay Vidyadharan, Supriyo Sircar, and Sunish Raj. The work was partially supported by the National Science Foundation [Grants 0943215 and 0943151], VOSS Program and by McIntire Summer Research Grants.

Contents

List of Figures

List of Tables

CHAPTER 1

Work–Life Balance: An Overview

Introduction

Over the last few decades, activities that are formally recognized as "work" have increasingly become important to the sustenance of individuals to an extent that they are seen as encroaching upon other essential aspects of their existence. Much of this encroachment has been due to work being viewed as a virtue in and of itself, the constant introduction of new technologies that have resulted in a blurring of work and life boundaries, and a general trend in which employees are increasingly having to take on a broader set of responsibilities (Poelmans et al., 2009). Recognizing the potentially negative effects of such pressures, employee well-being has gradually entered the vocabulary of workforce management and ensuring employee well-being is becoming an organizational imperative.

The definitions of work originate in diverse disciplines such as philosophy, sociology, and physics, and are hence unsurprisingly elusive. Without complicating matters and attempting to reconcile the various conceptualizations and definitions, we operationally view *work* undertaken by an individual as purposefully fulfilling certain responsibilities and carrying out duties that require sustained physical or mental effort, often "under compulsion or necessity" (e.g., for wages to sustain life). On the other hand, *life*, refers to "nonwork" aspects including "family, social, and spiritual" dimensions of the individual's existence (Poelmans et al., 2009).

S. Sarker et al., *Navigating Work and Life Boundaries*,
https://doi.org/10.1007/978-3-030-72759-8_1

Early conceptualizations of work and life viewed these as "competing priorities in a zero-sum game" (Friedman et al., 2000, p. 1). As some societies have changed such that "[h]aving a highly paid job and career no longer seem to be the most important and central objectives," individuals have started striving for a more "complete life" with both a "successful professional life and a personal life" (Poelmans et al., 2009, pp. 182–183). This turn led to the popularity of the notion of *balancing* work and life in the late 1970s and 80s, particularly in the United Kingdom and the United States.

One of the terms related to the above that has become popular is *work–life balance* (WLB), which has been defined in many ways in the literature. For example, a broad definition used by many scholars is that WLB represents "the relationship between the institutional and cultural times and spaces of work and nonwork in societies where income is predominantly generated and distributed through labor markets" (Felstead et al., 2002, p. 56). This definition stems from the view of employment as a "purchase of workers' time and presence," but only for a part of a day or week or year (Felstead et al., 2002). Time during which a worker is employed is seen to have boundaries, and for any worker to have a wholesome existence, the extent of time within the work boundary and process of transitioning across the boundaries need to be managed (e.g., Felstead et al., 2002).

What Does "Balance" Mean?

An important aspect of the WLB concept is the emphasis on the word "balance"—it refers to "a state in which different things occur in equal or proper amounts or have an equal or proper amount of importance" ("balance," n.d.). In the context of WLB, the term suggests an implicit belief that work and life represent two very different, perhaps opposing domains of an individual's existence. The underlying idea is that an individual needs leisure and time for nonwork activities, and their life would become dysfunctional without a suitable proportion of leisure and nonwork activities to complement the individual's involvement in work. Nord et al. view work–life balance "as a sort of an *equilibrium*... between the demands of work with those of their lives beyond the workplace" (2002, p. 223, italics added). Poelmans et al. emphasize the same idea viewing it as the "balance of work responsibilities and non-work responsibilities" (2009, p. 187). Highlighting the idea of conflict as being opposed to harmony (as reflected above) which appears to be equated to balance in much of the literature, Poelmans et al. (2009, p. 187) note that scholars such as Clark (2000) see WLB as being "at the opposite end of the work-Life Conflict [WLC] spectrum"—that is, balance and conflict are positioned at two opposite ends of a continuum. Bringing focus on the roles one has in work and nonwork spaces, rather than just on the tussle for time to be dedicated to the two aspects of existence, Clark (2000, p. 751) sees balance as "good functioning at work and home, with a minimum of role conflict." Kossek and Lee (2017) view work–life balance and conflict as being "conceptually overlapping" because each of them "implies the absence of the other." Hill et al. (2001, p. 49) further elaborate on the nature of demands faced by individuals in balancing as "the temporal, emotional and behavioral demands of both paid work and family responsibility." Somewhat consistent with the above, Kalliath and Brough (2008) hold that in the context of work and life, balance can be *time-related*, *involvement-related*, and *satisfaction-related*.

A study by Hoffman and Cowan (2008) explored the idea of balance from a rhetorical perspective. They used rhetorical analysis to "examine organizational Web sites in order to identify the ideology of work/life promoted by contemporary organizations" (p. 229). Their data highlighted that "at first glance, 'balance' seems to suggest a *healthy mix* of work and other concerns," however, a detailed reading revealed that "balance represents work and life as *two equal halves* of an equation, even though work is traditionally thought of as occupying only 40 of the total 168 hours in a week" (p. 234). Along these above lines, a number of perspectives on balance emerged from our interviews with IT workers, consultants, and managers around the globe that we briefly present below. This qualitative data was gathered from two different data collection efforts: (1) The first was an exploratory and interpretive case study of a leading global company headquartered in the United States. The division we studied was involved in designing/developing information systems that helped to manage client relationships. This division consisted of offshore employees (primarily developers) located in India and some in China as well as some project managers, clients, and a Division Head located in the United States; and (2) a set of interviews with IT consultants and managers from leading IT offshoring companies such as Wipro, Cognizant, IBM Consulting, LG, to name only a few, located in India, China, Korea, United Kingdom, and Scandinavia (see Appendix Table A.1 for details of the data collection).

Balance as Maintaining Life and Work Domain Separation

Something striking was that some of our respondents indeed appeared to echo Friedman et al.'s (2000, p. 1) view of work and life "as competing priorities"; for them, achieving balance was closely related to separation of the life and work domains, so that both domains have their place in the individual's existence but the possibility of work encroaching upon personal life is avoided at all costs. By having well-defined boundaries, usually based on time and place, a healthy but static mix is maintained, that helps achieve balance. In the words of an IT worker:

> I want a 9 to 5 job. I don't care if I don't get promoted in five years ... I'll do whatever you give me between 9 and 5. Don't give me an assignment outside of that.

Another IT worker held the following view about balance between work and life domains:

> To me, it's being able to let go at the end of the day and 100% invest my concentration, my time, my happiness into my family or leisure activity, or hobby or flat [apartment] where I'm not thinking about work to any degree.

Leslie et al. refer to such a view as more of a "fixed-pie" ideology where the IT worker believes that a "finite set of psychological and physical resources exist" (2019, p. 74), and some of the resources need to be dedicated to work (from 9–5 pm), and the rest of the resources should belong to life.

Balance as a Compromise

Some of the other respondents indicated that balance for them was a well-reasoned, pragmatic arrangement, something that they settled with or conceded to, keeping larger interests in mind, such as making a good living. For example, a Senior Firmware Engineer reflected on WLB as follows:

> ...I was doing this kind of work before I got married. And so, it was kind of an expectation at that time, that this is my life and you can accept it or not, but this is the way it's going to be. [Since getting married...] it's

> never, it's never…[been] been an antagonistic situation, because like I say, I have a wife who is very supportive, and…as the sole breadwinner in our family, she knows that it's important for me to keep my job.

A senior developer offered his view about some of the IT workers in India whom he had interacted with:

> My perspective about how work-life balance is in India…For most people I have interacted with, work is much more prioritized than life is…time out with family, friends, or going out on vacations, stuff like that is low [priority].

The above quote represents a perspective adopted by many employees that may not necessarily be the most desirable but necessary to meet other goals in life. Leslie et al. refer to such a philosophy as work priority ideology where workers believe that their "work is more important than their personal life" (2019, p. 75). The quote also highlights the view that the national context can influence the definition of work–life balance for an individual.

Another type of compromise that became evident from our interviews is when one member of the family, often the woman in traditional societies such as India, has to make professional sacrifices for the sake of balance. For example, a lab services and solutions team member said:

> I've seen a lot of people, my own colleagues' wives in good positions in the IT industry, give up their jobs…So if you ask me, between men and women, where I think that the problem remains, especially in India, [when] the compromise happens, the woman makes the compromise…

Balance as Joint Optimization

Some of the respondents also highlighted the fact that an optimal nature and amount of work and life activities are needed for an individual to maintain balance between the two domains. An application developer reflected on his view of balance as follows:

> To me [balance between work and life] means the ability to interweave my work.. and the rest of my life in such a way that both are optimized and neither suffers.

A technical lead also appeared to have a similar view:

> I think work-life balance is where I can give the fullest to both....My personal life should not interfere with my professional nor should my professional interfere with my personal. I hopefully will enjoy both of them.

Frone (2003) suggests that "high levels of inter-role facilitation" (p. 145) are required to achieve such joint optimization. The theme of facilitation, a delicate and dynamic process, is underscored by one of our interviewees, a female IT worker, who stated:

> We are measuring [evaluating] together – how do you facilitate, how do you have [both]... the company values your time and your responsibility that you have to spend towards your work as well as personal life? And, you know, so they know what is expected of you at work and understand what is expected of you in personal life and facilitate that delicate [prioritization]. Indeed, in many parts of the world, such facilitation is inherent in most companies given the societal values and assumptions about work and leisure.

We notice that facilitation allocates some of the responsibilities to managers, rather than leave the entire responsibility to the employee. Friedman et al. (2000, pp. 1–2) offer three principles for facilitation: First, managers need to be clear in informing employees about organization's work-related needs and priorities, and simultaneously encourage employees to articulate their own personal nonwork needs and priorities. Second, managers need to "recognize and support their employees as whole people" (Friedman et al., 2000, p. 1) ensuring that both work and non-work needs are being accommodated and actually celebrated. Third, they need to "continually experiment" the way tasks are allocated and accomplished, such that iteratively, work and nonwork needs are met optimally.

Balance as Integration

> Increasingly, many employees, especially in the Information Technology sector, are recognizing the futility of separating their work and nonwork domains, and, thus, they see balance as referring to the state of integration

between the domains, such that separate accounting of time, psychological involvement, or effort dedicated toward work and nonwork activities would not remain feasible or even meaningful. For example, an IT worker reflected on her experiences in the following way:

> I feel like my work and life is integrated. It's not an isolation...because when you go back home work just doesn't stop. You might end up with one or two calls...So it's kind of very, very intervening. If you do work at home and you probably pick up a kid and go on and attend a concert and then you attend the concert and then you come back and work.

Yet another individual offered the opinion that integration was more appropriate than balance for his profession, highlighting the social nature of knowledge work wherein nonwork activities (e.g., discussion on baseball with system client) is intertwined with work (e.g., systems analysis):

> The way I perceive it, if I start distinguishing between the work-only and the personal-life...that will certainly create a problem. I mean the problem for myself...I try to seek life in work...So working with people, making friends at workplace, interacting with client. I never see client as only the person who assigns me work. Rather as a friend. We talk about the baseball and my current client is a US baseball [fan] So it's not only work...And...what happens, ultimately this creates a kind of positive energy. If you're happy at work, you're happy at home. If you're happy at home, you're happy at work.

Having seen the different ways in which practitioners in the field view "balance," we briefly review some theoretical perspectives on Work–Life Balance (WLB) and Work–Life Conflict (WLC). As we mentioned earlier, we consider these concepts as *polar opposites on the same continuum* (that is, the *lack of balance* equates to *conflict*).

Approaches to Managing and Theorizing About WLB/WLC[1]

Prior studies on Work–Life Balance (WLB) and Work–Life Conflict (WLC[2]) have approached the concepts, their antecedents, and their consequences either from an organizational or an individual-level perspective. It is worth noting here that not all scholars in the area see the absence of balance as conflict (and vice versa), and they argue for the two constructs to be considered as independent (Kossek & Lee, 2017). For example, Poelmans et al. (2009) argue that it is possible for an individual to have balance, defined in some objective way such as allocation of time, and yet face conflict. While we do see merit in these arguments, for our purposes in this book, we feel comfortable in adopting the mainstream position of ***work–life conflict and work–life balance being viewed as related but opposing concepts*** (e.g., Kossek & Lee, 2017).

Organizational level researchers tend to focus on the "adoption of work-life balance practices" by organizations (Felstead et al., 2002, p. 57). For example, adaptation theorists argue that organizations seek to interpret the "changing world" around them, and it is this sense-and-response mechanism that drives management to implement different work–life balance programs (Felstead et al., 2002, p. 57). Other organizational-level researchers have recommended "lessons for effective implementation" of work–life balance programs (e.g., Nord et al., 2002, p. 223). The overall goal of many such programs is (among others) to "raise employee commitment to the organization" (Felstead et al., 2002, p. 58) by, for instance, introducing dependent care, allowing flexible and remote work, and having provisions for part-time work with no compulsion to work overtime respectively. Past research confirms linkages between the specific variables such as "employees' perceptions of support, flexibility, overload, or a family supportive organizational culture" and WLC, though it is not clear how the favorable perceptions among employees may be created (Kelly et al., 2008, p. 312).

[1] A significant proportion of the text in this section is taken from Sarker, S., Ahuja, M., & Sarker, S. (2018). Work–life conflict of globally distributed software development personnel: An empirical investigation using border theory. *Information Systems Research, 29*(1), 103–126. Permission secured.

[2] Some bodies of work use the term "work-family conflict" which we subsume within "work-life conflict." Life includes not only family, but also friends, personal interests and so on; nevertheless, the two terms are often used interchangeably (Kossek & Lee, 2017).

Researchers examining the issue of WLB from the *individual employees' standpoint* generally focus on explaining why certain individuals experience high WLC, and on unearthing the tactics and resources that can be used by the employees in an effort to improve on their balance. Factors identified include demographics, personality, family circumstances, and so on. We will discuss several of the factors in this group in Chapters 2 and 3.

Different researchers also frame the management of WLB/WLC differently, in the form of *five different models* that have a distinct foci but do have overlaps (Guest, 2002; Zedeck & Mosier, 1990). First is the *segmentation model*, which argues that "work and non-work are two distinct domains of life that are lived quite separately and have no influence on each other" (Guest, 2002, p. 258). The *spillover model* on the other hand rejects this segmentation view, and holds that there are ample spillovers between these two domains, and researchers adhering to this view focus on understanding what causes the spillovers, and the nature of these spillovers. Spillover models suggest that the time during which a worker is employed "has boundaries," and are "juxtaposed to non-work times and places," and it is important to understand the point of transitioning (that is, the shift from the work space-time to the non-work space-time) and to manage the process of transitioning (Felstead et al., 2002). The *compensation model* argues that whatever an individual lacks in one domain in terms of satisfaction or demand is made up in the other domain. Finally, the *instrumental model* argues that certain activities in one domain can actually be used to "facilitate success" in the other domain, and the model attempts to understand how such facilitation can be done.

While each of the above models has merit, perhaps the *conflict model* best fits with the primary context of our interest, that is IT work and more broadly all forms of knowledge work that occurs in contemporary organizations, that are often global and distributed in nature. This model holds that the high demands of the modern globalized economy cause significant conflicts between one's work and life domains, which are unavoidable. Researchers supporting the conflict model attempt to understand the types of conflict, the antecedents and effects of this conflict, and how they may be reduced (Greenhaus & Beutell, 1985; Guest, 2002). Kossek et al. (1999, p. 103), for example, emphasize that proponents of the conflict model typically assess "the sources, processes and types of conflict between work and family roles and their consequences for attitudinal outcomes." Given the temporal, spatial, and cultural distances with colleagues and clients that IT professionals engaged in software development have to continuously bridge (Kotlarsky & Oshri, 2005; Oshri et al., 2008; Sarker & Sahay, 2004), we would expect that they experience significant conflicts (i.e., tensions) between their work and nonwork domains.

The conflict model typically approaches the relationship between work and life as having "inter-role conflict where the demands created by the job interfere with performing family-related responsibilities" (Netemeyer et al., 2004, p. 50). Quick et al. (2004, p. 428) argue that the discord with respect to an individual's ability to manage time and attention between work and nonwork can lead to an increased level of WLC. These authors also argue that two important factors (or conflicts) that hinder the balance between one's work and life are time-based conflict and strain-based conflict. While the two types of conflicts are sometimes difficult to demarcate, *time-based conflict* refers to the discord that arises when "the time devoted to work makes it difficult to fulfill the obligations and requirements of the family role" (Quick et al., 2004, p. 428). For example, staying late at the office (or working late) prevents an employee from attending family activities (such as an evening meal together). In other words, time spent by the employee in one domain (in this case, work) prevents him/her from spending time on the other domain (in this case, home or family). In contrast, *strain-based conflict* arises when the "pressures of the work role" spillover and "affect interactions within the family domain" (Quick et al., 2004, p. 428). Such conflicts can put an employee in a perpetual bad mood, and result in negative interactions with his/her family. In the context of IT work arrangements, we believe that both these types of conflicts are likely to be present among employees. Given that much of the IT work unfolds in global arrangements, employees in a development center at a particular geographical location are expected to regularly collaborate and coordinate their activities with employees at the overseas centers. Significant time differences between these centers mandate the need for employees in one (or both) locations to stretch their work times, thereby creating conflicts with their family times (see Chapter 5 for a detailed case study). Similarly, working in distributed networks across time, space, working styles, and culture (Krishna et al., 2004; Sarker & Sahay, 2004) can give rise to frustrations and stress due to lack of a shared frame of reference, different interpretations of the same fact, and incomplete understanding of the capabilities and constraints of team members in other locations, all of which results in spilling over of the strain to the nonwork or family domains. Kossek and Lee (2017) alert us to yet another type of conflict, that of behavior-based conflict. Some professions might require more "aggressive interpersonal interactions" (e.g., military) that might not lend itself well to positive "family interactions." While such conflict may not be always applicable to IT or other forms of knowledge work, tough decisions and choices that leaders make even in such environments (e.g., firing other employees) may result in an adversarial effect seeping into the family domain.

Another theoretical perspective sees work–life conflict as stress that arises within their *conservation of resources*. The conservation of resources perspective assumes that individuals always strive to gain and preserve different types of resources, and conflict arises when there is either a threat of loss of the available resources or when the resources expended do not produce the expected results. Greenblatt (2002) takes a somewhat similar approach and suggests that work–life conflicts can be reduced by "obtaining and managing sufficient resources" (p. 179). The three types of relevant resources outlined by Greenblatt (2002, p. 179) are (1) temporal resources, (2) financial resources, and (3) control. Temporal resources refer to the availability of time, for both official and personal purposes; financial resources refer to the existence of money to buy goods and services that can help achieve "life satisfaction"; and finally, control refers to the freedom "to select when and how to create important outcomes." While financial resources may not be an important criterion affecting the IT workforce (since most IT workers tend to be fairly well-paid), both time and control can be critical for reducing the conflict between work and life in the context of knowledge work. There might be feelings of burnout when an individual spends a large amount of time-related resources at work that takes away precious time from family and nonwork activities.

Yet another theoretical view related to resources is the *job demands-and-resources model* which assumes that "job demands may deplete individuals' resources, resulting in negative individual and work outcomes" (Kossek & Lee, 2017). This paradigm emphasizes the importance of factors such as autonomy, supportive supervisor, among others as critical resources that contribute to a better WLB. Further, an important element of this theory is the idea of fit, which is seen to be achieved when the existing resources satisfy the demand. For example, during a crunch period when the IT worker is facing significant "demands" at work, a supportive and understanding family or fewer responsibilities can be seen as a higher amount of "resource availability," thereby creating a "fit" and reducing perceptions of WLC. On the contrary, during such high demand times, inflexible expectations of fulfilling family commitment (and less availability of individual's autonomy-related resources) would be considered a poor fit (at that time), and thus increase conflict.

Moving away from the idea of resources, Elder (1998) proposed the life-course perspective. This takes a more contextual and networked perspective and views WLC as shifting with the period a society is in, and the phase of life of the worker. Along these lines, today's young IT worker, with suitable skills, is likely to demand more flexible hours from their employers, and focus on more arrangements (e.g., domestic help) to ensure that they lead a more balanced life. Further, WLC for the same generation of workers, even in the same organization, will likely depend on the lifecycle phase of the worker. For example, a worker with an adolescent child is likely to face different demands and challenges compared to those faced by their colleague who has a newborn. Finally, the life-course perspectives' emphasis on networked effects highlights the point that an IT worker with a stay-at-home partner is likely to face very different types of conflict than one whose partner also works in a similar job environment.

While we have reviewed a number of theoretical perspectives on WLB/WLC, we hope the reader would agree that they do not provide a broad frame to study the phenomenon holistically and systematically, focusing on the antecedents and consequences of WLB or WLC. With this in mind, we next discuss a theoretical perspective, that we believe is generative, and can guide the systematic and relatively comprehensive investigation of this phenomenon in our context of interest.

Border Theory: Conceptualizing the Work and Life Domains as Different Nations with Borders

Border Theory and its derivatives have been used in a number of disciplines, most frequently, within the domain of political science and international relations. Brunet-Jailly (2006) presented this theory to explain the underlying complications that are faced by borderland cities including the impact that local environments and multiple levels of the government have on these cities. Since this work was published, Border Theory has been used to understand complexities related to national borders, exchanges of information, and political clout across borders (Navarrette et al., 2009). Within the domain of political science and governmental studies, Border Theory highlights that the two important components contributing to the complications are: (1) *the agency*, referring to individuals and their beliefs, values, motivations, etc., and (2) *the structures*, referring to institutional and social forces that shape the individual actions and beliefs (e.g. Navarrete et al., 2009).

What makes Border Theory particularly relevant to studying WLB/WLC, especially in IT-related work? While it is often said that there is never a perfect theory and that "theory is our chronically inadequate attempt to come to terms with the infinite complexity of the real world" (Walsham, 1997, p. 478), the notions of "border" and "border crossing" and the challenges "border crossers" face in Border Theory, appear well-suited to examining our phenomenon of interest, namely IT or knowledge workers. In this context, individuals have to constantly negotiate the borders related to work and life domains as well as place and time (e.g., Sarker et al., 2012). This is especially the situation since in today's world, much of IT work, whether related to application development or IT implementation, is managed by distributed teams where the clients, project managers, and developers might be in different cities or even different countries. Indeed, we found that a small number of articles have used this theory to examine issues related to organizational employees and their well-being (please see Appendix Table A.4 for a review of this literature). As noted earlier, this body of work was inspired by and developed from Lewin's (1966) "conception of regions divided by boundaries within the employee's lifespace" (Lambert et al., 2006, p. 67).

While relatively new, this theoretical perspective is gaining popularity among WLB/WLC researchers. Similar to the way Border Theory is used in political science, in the context of organizational employees, the theory holds that work and life are two different "domains," much like two different countries. The domains, like countries, are seen to differ in "purpose and culture" (Clark, 2000, p. 751)—in how tasks are accomplished, and in acceptable codes of conduct. It should be noted that, in the context of this book, not only do individuals have separate domains of work and life, but also their work domains may consist of two or more sub-domains, that of their own location, and those of their remote colleagues with whom they need to interact and collaborate on a regular basis. Thus, IT workers find themselves constantly crossing borders not only between work and life but also within their work domains (much like daily commuters between Germany and Switzerland, for example, do in the physical world). Thus, Border Theory provides an appropriate lens to understand this complex context, and to derive a more holistic understanding of the antecedents and effects of such frequent border crossing.

The focus of Border Theory, then, is *to understand how the individuals make the transition between their different domains*. For some individuals, the "transition is slight," as in a transition between two neighboring or culturally similar countries (Clark, 2000, p. 751). For many others, and arguably the ones in the IT context, the transitions are larger, and therefore more difficult. Border Theory helps us understand how individuals tailor their domains and build "bridges" between the domains in an effort to achieve balance (Clark, 2000, p. 751). Given the similarities between national border crossing and work–life border crossing, Border Theory *points to a number of categories of variables that are not self-evident*, and need to be deliberately considered in order to gain a holistic understanding of the phenomenon of interest. To elaborate, in line with Clark (2000), we map the concepts in Border Theory to work–life balance issues. First, is the concept of the *border* itself, which are "lines of demarcation between the domains" (Clark, 2000, p. 756), and which highlights where one domain ends and the other starts. Borders can primarily be physical and temporal, and sometimes borders can end up being fuzzy (e.g., Bennett et al., 2006). *Physical borders* are similar to walls that create a distinction between or among domains. For example, in the case of a distributed team member, there are physical borders between his/her *work* and *home* locations, and between the locations of their work and those of remote colleagues. *Temporal borders* are time-related distinctions from one domain to another. For the IT worker, temporal border includes the *time-zone differences* between the individual and their remote colleagues. It could also be distinction between work time and family time.

A second core construct of Border Theory is the *border crosser*, that is, the focal individual who transitions between the work and life domains. According to border theorists (e.g., Clark, 2000; Lambert et al., 2006), personal attributes (e.g., gender, personality), and extent of domain responsibilities (e.g., family, dependents) can play an important role in influencing a border crosser's WLB (e.g., Clark, 2002; Donald & Linington, 2008).

Clark also discusses two *border-related characteristics* that play key roles. They are the *permeability* of the border and the *flexibility* of the border. Permeability may be defined as the "degree to which elements from other domains may enter the current domain" (Clark, 2000, p. 756). More specifically, it may be seen as the "degree to which each domain allows the psychological concerns of one domain to enter the physical location of others [the other domain]" (Cowan & Hoffman, 2007, p. 38). Permeability might refer to work concerns (e.g., emails) and meetings that may seep into personal time, and vice versa. While work and life domains tend to be fairly distinct for many individuals, sometimes there are specific factors within the work domain that may cause spillovers to the life domain, and vice versa. Flexibility of the border may be defined as the "extent to which a border may contract or expand, depending on the demands of one domain over another" (Clark, 2000, p. 757). In other words, it refers to the malleability of the borders between the two domains, and the extent to which the borders can be legitimately stretched. Flexible work schedules are seen as bringing about flexibility of the border (e.g., Cowan & Hoffman, 2007; Lambert et al., 2006). Scholars observe that borders having high permeability and flexibility can lead to "blending," thereby creating a "borderland" that does not belong to either domain (Clark, 2000, p. 757). Borderlands have been found to result in negative consequences with respect to WLB since it is a space where the border crossers find themselves caught between conflicting demands.

Border Theory also suggests that the *domain members* play important roles (e.g., Clark, 2000; Lambert et al., 2006). Among the domain members are *border keepers*, who not only define the domains, but also manage them—these include supervisors as well as the organizational policies surrounding work and life (e.g., Greeff, 2000). Clark (2002) argued that border keepers usually have power over the border crosser. In addition, the border crosser may be *reliant on or connected to other domain members*. Finally, the *characteristics of the domain itself* have been found to be relevant (Clark, 2000).

As the review of the existing studies on Border Theory within organizational domain highlights (see Appendix Table A.4), Border Theory has been used rather loosely in the past, with authors basing their model development or theoretical arguments on the basic premise that organizational employees are border crossers transitioning between the work and family countries on a daily basis, and that the characteristics of these domains, the flexibility of these borders, and the border crossers' own characteristics, have an effect. While Clark (2000) provides some specific instantiations, for the most part, Border Theory provides only the broad categories, not specific variables. Another notable point from our review is that studies that have drawn upon Border Theory have been primarily theoretical in nature, and, in cases where the studies have included any empirical analysis, those have involved surveys of general employees with a generic set of variables, which does little to inform readers about specific contexts such as IT work, and how such work might affect WLB. For example, while permeability may be viewed as important, it is not obvious how permeability might be relevant to the context of an IT worker collaborating with remote colleagues on a software development project. As we mentioned earlier, *the characteristics of the domain itself were found to be important by border theorists* (Clark, 2000).

Key Impacts of Work–Life Conflict Highlighted in the Context of Information Systems

While the focus of much of the literature has been on the factors, typically antecedents, that cause or mitigate WLC, it is also important to assess the impacts of WLC on individuals and sometimes even the organization in which an individual may be embedded. The question here is, why is WLC important for individuals and organizations? A short answer to this question is that in most cases, WLC is undesirable for both the individuals and their organizations. For example, WLC is known to influence "*work outcomes*" which often refer to "individual-level employee attitudes and behaviors on the job" such as job satisfaction (negatively), organizational commitment (negatively), and turnover intentions (positively); further, these work outcomes may include stress, "job [or task] performance and absenteeism" (Kelly et al., 2008, p. 311), where stress and absenteeism is known to go up and performance goes down. Such *individual-level outcomes* could also impact "*business outcomes*" such as cost, ROI, and revenues (p. 312). Furthermore, consequences could negatively influence family and other social relationships, by precipitating divorce and social alienation, which could then influence work as well as business outcomes. In the table below, we summarize some of the negative consequences of WLC within the IT sector, as assessed from our interviews (Table 1.1).

We must note here that while our orientation in this book is that WLB is desirable and the consequences of high WLC are likely to be negative, it is worth keeping in mind that the interaction between work and family domains can sometimes lead to "work–life enrichment" rather

Table 1.1 Some of the impacts of high work–life conflict (WLC)

Impact	*Definitions*	*Quotes/anecdotes from interviews*
Turnover/Turnover Intentions	The behavior of "leaving [the] organization" (Armstrong et al., 2007) ".. voluntary turnover intention is defined as a conscious and deliberate willingness to leave one's formal organization of employment" (Lo, 2015)	"I did twenty-four products for them in one-and-half years… building me as a professional, it was great, but work life balance.. I won't [could not] stand it anymore. That is the reason why I left the company… I want my life back." "I have seen a lot of women in the past quit because they simply can't handle.. work [and life], and balance both of them" "I think it is a problem that we really need to look at… we are hearing a lot of cases, right, of people at forty, some of our own colleagues… it is all due to stress.. and that's what is going to happen… attrition."
Job Satisfaction	"The extent of positive emotional response to the job resulting from an employee's appraisal of the job as fulfilling or congruent with the individual's values (Morris & Venkatesh, 2010; Weiss & Cropanzano, 1996)" (Tripp et al., 2016, p. 271)	"For me personally, I enjoy doing what I am doing, so I am not really working" "..this one team, which I know has, for a long time, been working long hours.. I think it has been for more than a year, but if you meet them you will never think they are burnt out. They are.. so passionate about the work that they are doing.."

(continued)

Table 1.1 (continued)

Impact	*Definitions*	*Quotes/anecdotes from interviews*
Stress	"Situation wherein job-related factors interact with a worker to change (i.e. disrupt or enhance) his or her psychological and/or physiological condition such that the person (i.e., mind-body) is forced to deviate from normal functioning" (Beehr & Newman, 1978, p. 670)	"I think stress levels are pretty high… because they are pulled into a lot of calls, a lot of discussion locally as well as globally" "..the balance comes where I am not having to juggle priorities and this..[reduces].. stress.. For me stress is created when the priorities are not where they ought to be.."
Health Problems	These may include hypertension, burnout, heart disease, psychological distress, depression, etc. (Kelly et al. 2008)	"[Working] 16-18 hours [a day] took a hit on my personal life and health and every aspect of it …" "I do not want my team-members to get burnt out because of work … I tell people, 'you are working too hard. Get out".. that is something I do
Valence	"the degree of attractiveness an individual, activity, or thing possesses as a behavioral goal", which could be toward the IS profession or distributed software development or offshoring (Merriam Webster, also consistent with Vroom's Expectancy Theory (1964) Sarker et al. (2010)	"I am really focused on my career I feel like I am doing really good.." One of our respondents talked about a former colleague leaving the profession of IT consulting and settling in a rural setting as a farmer, owing to the very awful experience in the industry
Task Performance/job performance	How well the given individual accomplishes the task assigned or handles their responsibilities	"I feel that the quality of what I produce is better when I have.. a balanced life" "we have to be very cognizant of the fact that people have to maintain their work-life balance otherwise they cannot be productive"

than conflict. Greenhaus and Powell (2006, p. 76), for instance, discuss a number of mechanisms including "positive spillovers" (e.g., having a good day at work can make one deal with home issues more positively, and having "love and respect" of one's family can make one feel "confident.. at work") that can contribute to such enrichment. Furthermore, some scholars such as Perrigino et al. (2018) remind us that there is a "dark side" to reducing WLC. In other words, policies that seek to enhance WLB (or reduce WLC) can lead to a "backlash" (Perrigino et al., 2018, p. 600)—these may arise through a number of mechanisms, including *inequity mechanisms* (e.g., childless employees might view childcare facilities on company premises as serving the interest of employees with young children but not them), *stigma mechanisms* (e.g., asking for paternity leave might be viewed negatively by supervisors and colleagues), *spillover mechanisms* (e.g., employees' inability to disconnect from work that leads to worsening of WLC due to implementation of technology-mediated remote work, originally intended to reduce WLC), and *strategic mechanisms* (e.g., an organization's implementation of policies to reduce WLC may be seen as "window dressing," possibly due to "mimetic pressures" being faced by it) (Perrigino et al., 2018, p. 604). Some of these mechanisms such as spillovers due to technology-mediated remote work are being witnessed currently in the world today due to the COVID-induced work from home practices. The ramification of the above is that the implementation of policies in organizations should involve careful reflection regarding the potentially negative, sometimes unanticipated "attitudes," "emotions," and "behaviors" that can arise among employees (p. 600).

Looking Ahead

In this chapter, we have offered an overview of the key terms and concepts, and some theoretical models related to the phenomenon of interest. We have introduced the readers to Border Theory that has been used primarily in Political Science and International Relations to study issues around national borders—this appears to have much relevance in understanding and explaining the complex notion of Work–Life Balance (WLB) and Work–Life Conflict (WLC). We also briefly discussed some negative consequences of high WLC (or low WLB) and alerted readers to also keep in mind the "dark side" of WLB.

In Chapter 2, we contextualize Border Theory the work and life domains within the primary context of interest, that of IT work conducted in globally distributed teams. This contextualization, while focusing on the specific task of software development, is applicable more broadly to distributed teams engaged in knowledge work such as consulting, design, and development that require specific skills often concentrated in different locations, and coordination across space and time.

Chapter 3 focuses on individual-level factors (i.e., those pertaining to the border crosser) that have been discussed in the traditional literature in the context of WLC. Our goal is to revisit and empirically examine some of these factors in the context of globally distributed IT work. For example, does gender make a difference in the level of WLC these professionals experience and perceive? Do certain personality characteristics such as neuroticism matter? Does valuing leisure time matter? Chapter 4 drills deeper into the context of globally distributed IT work, specifically that of offshore insourcing, by exploring the changing nature of relationships between the onshore and offshore sites, and how the changing WLC considerations influence issues such as task responsibilities, identity, and control associated with the sites. Some unusual dilemmas surrounding the management of offshore workforce's WLC issues emerge. Chapter 5 explores the effects of personal mobile devices on the WLC of IT workers and consultants. Three worldviews or conceptions of these IT workers and consultants regarding the relationship between their work and life domains emerged from the study, and a number of organizational or managerial strategies to manage the WLC concerns of employees with the different worldviews were discerned. The key message of this chapter is that there is no single strategy that is likely to work for all employees in any organization, and that it behooves organizations to offer a menu of options to allow for individual preferences. Finally, Chapter 6 provides a summary of some of the key insights discussed in Chapters 2–5, and it concludes with a discussion on how the COVID pandemic, resulting in a simultaneous stay and work from home situation for a large proportion of the population, has made many of the themes of managing borders as part of distributed IT or knowledge work relevant to the broader population.

References

Armstrong, D. J., Riemenschneider, C., Reid, M., & Allen, M. (2007). Voluntary turnover and women in IT: A cognitive study of work-family conflict. *Information & Management, 44*(2), 142–153.

balance. (n.d.). In Merriam-Webster.com. Retrieved June 28, 2020, from https://www.merriam-webster.com/dictionary/balance.

Beehr, T. A., & Newman, J. E. (1978). Job stress, employee health, and organizational effectiveness: A facet analysis, model, and literature review. *Personnel Psychology, 31*(4), 665–699.

Bennett, J. B., Patterson, C. R., Witala, W., & Woo, A. (2006). Social risks for atrisk drinking in young workers: Application of work-life border theory. *Journal of Drug Issues, 36*(3), 485–514.

Brunet-Jailly, E. (2006). Security and border security policies: Perimeter or smart border? A comparison of the European Union and Canadian-American border security regimes. *Journal of Borderlands Studies, 21*(1), 3–21.

Clark, S. C. (2000). Work/family border theory: A new theory of work/family balance. *Human Relations, 53*(6), 747–770.

Clark, S. C. (2002). Communicating across the work/home border. *Community Work Family, 5*(1), 23–48.

Cowan, R. L., & Hoffman, M. F. (2007). The flexible organization: How contemporary employees construct the work/life border. *Qualitative Research Reports in Communication, 8*(1), 37–44.

Donald, F., & Linington, J. (2008). Work/family border theory and gender role orientation in male managers. *South African Journal of Psychology, 38*(4), 659–671.

Elder, G. H., Jr. (1998). The life course as developmental theory. *Child Development, 69*(1), 1–12.

Felstead, A., Jewson, N., Phizacklea, A., & Walters, S. (2002). Opportunities to work at home in the context of work-life balance. *Human Resource Management Journal, 12*(1), 54–76.

Friedman, S., Christensen, P., & Degroot, J. (2000). *Harvard business review on work and life balance*. Harvard Business Review.

Frone, M. R. (2003). Work–family balance. In J. C. Quick & L. E. Tetrick (Eds.), *Handbook of occupational health psychology* (pp. 143–162). American Psychological Association.

Greeff, A. P. (2000). Characteristics of families that function well. *Journal of Family Issues, 21*(8), 948–962.

Greenblatt, E. (2002). Work/life balance: Wisdom or whining. *Organizational Dynamics, 31*(2), 177–193.

Greenhaus, J. H., & Beutell, N. J. (1985). Sources of conflict between work and family roles. *Academy of Management Review, 10*(1), 76–88.

Greenhaus, J. H., & Powell, G. N. (2006). When work and family are allies: A theory of work-family enrichment. *Academy of Management Review, 31*(1), 72–92.

Guest, D. E. (2002). Perspectives on the study of work-life balance. *Social Science Information, 41*(2), 255–279.

Hill, E. J., Hawkins, A. J., Ferris, M., & Weitzman, M. (2001). Finding an extra day a week: The positive influence of perceived job flexibility on work and family life balance. *Family Relations, 50*(1), 49–58.

Hoffman, M. F., & Cowan, R. L. (2008). The meaning of work/life: A corporate ideology of work/life balance. *Communication Quarterly, 56*(3), 227–246.

Kalliath, T., & Brough, P. (2008). Work–life balance: A review of the meaning of the balance construct. *Journal of Management & Organization, 14*(3), 323–327.

Kelly, E. L., Kossek, E. E., Hammer, L. B., Durham, M., Bray, J., Chermack, K., & Kaskubar, D. (2008). Getting there from here: Research on the effects of work–family initiatives on work–family conflict and business outcomes. *Academy of Management Annals, 2*(1), 305–349.

Kossek, E. E., & Lee, K. H. (2017). Work-family conflict and work-life conflict. In *Oxford Research Encyclopedia of Business and Management*. https://doi.org/10.1093/acrefore/9780190224851.013.52.

Kossek, E. E., Noe, R., & DeMarr, B. J. (1999). Work-family role synthesis: Individual and organizational determinants. *International Journal of Conflict Management, 10*(2), 102.

Kotlarsky, J., & Oshri, I. (2005). Social ties, knowledge sharing and successful collaboration in globally distributed system development projects. *European Journal of Information Systems, 14*(1), 37–48.

Krishna, S., Sahay, S., & Walsham, W. (2004). Managing cross-cultural issues in global software outsourcing. *Communications of the ACM, 47*(4), 62–66.

Lambert, C. H., Kass, S. J., Piotrowski, C., & Vodanovich, S. J. (2006). Impact factors on work-family balance: Initial support for border theory. *Organization Development Journal, 24*(3), 64–75.

Leslie, L. M., King, E. B., & Clair, J. A. (2019). Work-life ideologies: The contextual basis and consequences of beliefs about work and life. *Academy of Management Review, 44*(1), 72–98.

Lewin, K. (1966). *Principles of topological psychology* (F. Heider & G. Heider, Trans.). McGraw-Hill.

Lo, J. (2015). The information technology workforce: A review and assessment of voluntary turnover research. *Information Systems Frontiers, 17*(2), 387–411.

Merriam-Webster. (n.d.). *Balance*. Retrieved June 28, 2020, from https://www.merriam-webster.com/dictionary/balance.

Merriam-Webster. (n.d.). *Work*. Retrieved June 28, 2020, from https://www.merriam-webster.com/dictionary/work.
Morris, M. G., & Venkatesh, V. (2010). Job characteristics and job satisfaction: Understanding the role of enterprise resource planning system implementation. *MIS Quarterly, 34*, 143–161.
Navarrete, A. C., Mellouli, S., Pardo, T. A., & Gil-Garcia, J. R. (2009). Information sharing at national borders: Extending the utility of border theory. *Proceedings of 42nd Hawaii International Conference on System Sciences*. IEEE Computing Society.
Netemeyer, R. G., Brashear-Alejandro, T., & Boles, J. S. (2004). A crossnational model of job-related outcomes of work role and family role variables: A retail sales context. *Journal of the Academy of Marketing Science, 32*(1), 49–60.
Nord, W. R., Fox, S., Phoenix, A., & Viano, K. (2002). Real-world reactions to work-life balance programs: Lessons for effective implementation. *Organizational Dynamics, 30*(3), 223–238.
Oshri, I., van Fenema, P. C., & Kotlarsky, J. (2008). Knowledge transfer in globally distributed teams: The role of transactive memory. In *Knowledge processes in globally distributed contexts* (pp. 24–52). Palgrave Macmillan.
Perrigino, M. B., Dunford, B. B., & Wilson, K. S. (2018). Work–family backlash: The "dark side" of work–life balance (WLB) policies. *Academy of Management Annals, 12*(2), 600–630.
Poelmans, S., Odle-Dusseau, H., & Beham, B. (2009). Work-life balance: Individual and organizational strategies and practices. In S. Cartwright & C. L. Cooper (Eds.), *The Oxford handbook of organizational well-being* (pp. 180–213). Oxford University Press.
Quick, J. D., Henley, A. B., & Quick, J. C. (2004). The balancing act–At work and at home. *Organizational Dynamics, 33*, 426–438.
Sarker, S., & Sahay, S. (2004). Implications of space and time for distributed work: An interpretive study of US–Norwegian systems development teams. *European Journal of Information Systems, 13*(1), 3–20.
Sarker, S., Sarker, S., & Jana, D. (2010). The impact of the nature of globally distributed work arrangement on WLC and valence. *European Journal of Information Systems, 19*(2), 209–222.
Sarker, S., Xiao, X., Sarker, S., & Ahuja, M. (2012). Managing employees' use of mobile technologies to minimize work-life balance impacts. *MIS Quart. Executive, 11*(4), 143–157.
Tripp, J. F., Riemenschneider, C., & Thatcher, J. B. (2016). Job satisfaction in agile development teams: Agile development as work redesign. *Journal of Association for Information Systems, 17*(4), 267–307.
Vroom, V. H. (1964). *Work and motivation*. Wiley.

Walsham, G. (1997). Actor-network theory and IS research: Current status and future prospects. In A. S. Lee, J. Liebenow, & J. I. DeGross (Eds.), *Information systems and qualitative research* (pp. 466–480). Chapman & Hall.

Weiss, H. M., & Cropanzano, R. (1996). Affective events theory: A theoretical discussion of the structure, causes and consequences of affective experiences at work. In B. M. Staw & L. L. Cummings (Eds.), *Research in organizational behavior: An annual series of analytical essays and critical reviews* (pp. 1–74). JAI Prees.

work. (n.d.). In Merriam-Webster.com. Retrieved June 28, 2020, from https://www.merriam-webster.com/dictionary/work.

Work-life balance. (n.d.). In *Wikipedia*. Retrieved June 28, 2020, from https://en.wikipedia.org/wiki/Work%E2%80%93life_balance.

Zedeck, S., & Mosier, K. L. (1990). Work in the family and employing organization. *American Psychologist, 45*(2), 240.

CHAPTER 2

The Antecedents of Work–Life Conflict in Distributed IT Work: *A Border Theory Perspective*

Introduction

In Chapter 1, we introduced Border Theory as a theoretical lens for examining work–life conflict (WLC).[1] In this chapter, we elaborate on different components of Border Theory and contextualize it within the globally distributed software development (GDSD) environment. Finally, we present an empirical examination of the relevant components of Border Theory in the globally distributed context. As we mentioned in Chapter 1, much of today's IT work (especially, software development) seeks to utilize expertise and talent from a global workforce and hence is often conducted in distributed settings.

An important question that may be asked is, what makes Border Theory particularly relevant to studying WLC in such contexts? While

[1] We note that for this book, as explained in Chapter 1, we consider high work-life conflict (WLC) as low work-life balance (WLB). In other words, the two constructs are seen as being on the same continuum, on opposing sides.

This Chapter presents a revised version of the paper: Sarker, S., Ahuja, M., & Sarker, S. (2018). Work–life conflict of globally distributed software development personnel: An empirical investigation using border theory. *Information Systems Research, 29*(1), 103–126.

S. Sarker et al., *Navigating Work and Life Boundaries*,
https://doi.org/10.1007/978-3-030-72759-8_2

"(t)here is not, and never will be, a best theory… [and noting that] theory is our chronically inadequate attempt to come to terms with the infinite complexity of the real world" (Walsham, 1997, p. 478), the notions of "border" and "border crossing" and the challenges "border crossers" face, in Border Theory, appear well-suited to examining IT work in globally distributed settings, wherein individuals must constantly negotiate the borders related to work and life domains but also between client and vendor firms, time zones, countries, and functional areas (e.g., Sarker et al., 2018). The unique nature of this type of work, which includes challenges such as long working hours, project complexity, separation by time and space, and potential for scope creep (Sarker et al., 2018), provides insights which can apply to many other types of work environments.

As discussed in Chapter 1, Border Theory provides several categories of variables starting with the border crosser (in this case, the IT worker), the characteristics of the border itself, border keepers (such as the organizational policies in which the IT professional works in), and characteristics of the domain in which the border crosser works in (e.g., IT work). We examined a large number of existing studies on WLB/WLC and found that: (1) only a handful of existing studies have adopted a border theory perspective, and none of them includes empirical examination, (2) limited work has been conducted on IT work especially in globally distributed settings, resulting in a huge gap in our understanding of this important context, and (3) the studies that have focused on WLC have tended to focus on the border crosser, leaving much to understand with respect to the role of the border keeper, the domain, and the characteristics of the border such as the temporality, physical border, flexibility, and permeability. We summarize some of the relevant literature in Appendix 2. The latter three categories (the role of the border keeper, the domain, and the nature of the work) are our focus of attention in this chapter. Another rationale for not focusing on characteristics of the Border Crossers as a starting point is that these variables are *a given* for the organization, and cannot be manipulated or easily changed (in the short run). Indeed, it might be considered discriminatory to "manipulate" some of the variables. That said, we do utilize some of the border crosser characteristics as *control variables* in the empirical examination presented later in this chapter, and examine them more independently in Chapter 3.

Building Our Research Model and Hypotheses

In identifying our specific variables of interest and in developing our research model, we utilized Border Theory and a large number of qualitative interviews with IT professionals from India, Europe, and United States, who work regularly in globally distributed settings (see Appendix 1). We also drew a great deal from research conducted in the domain of GDSD and other related areas.

Specifically, we incorporated micro theories and prior research in the areas of distributed work, WLB/WLC, software development, and employee–organization relationships to develop the hypotheses. For example, for understanding the impacts of the *locational and temporal distances* (or the physical and temporal borders) on WLC, we utilized *proximity theory*. For the role of the *border keepers*, we drew on the existing research in WLB/WLC, where much has been written about the role of the supervisor, and organizational policies. *Task interdependency theory* was used to predict the effect of *task reliance on other distributed members* on WLC, while extant literature on WLC and software development was used for understanding the role of the border characteristics such as flexibility and permeability.

Based on this work, we include seven categories of factors: extent of physical border as expressed through locational dispersion, extent of temporal border as manifested through time differences with remote members, flexibility of the border as evident from flexibility of schedules, permeability of the border manifested as the extent of use of agile methods, the border keeper's support as in the role of the organizational family friendly policies (FFPs) and supervisory support, dependency of the border crosser on remote members as manifested through the task interdependency, and the characteristics of the domain of software development work as one of the most dominant forms of IT work in remote settings) as captured through requirements instability, requirements diversity, and technological diversity. Table 2.1 shows some of the key variables identified within these categories.

Extent of the Physical Border: Locational Dispersion

As discussed earlier, Border Theory posits that physical borders (the physical lines of demarcation within which domain-related responsibilities are undertaken) play a key role in influencing the WLC of an individual.

Table 2.1 Sample variables that emerged from the case study

Variable suggested	*Category of the variable suggested by border theory*	*Sample quote*
Time difference	Extent of temporal border	[The] … biggest WLB challenge is the [lack of] time zone overlap … Sometimes [there were meetings] early morning and late night … Team 1 in the morning, and Team 2 in the evening, right. It kills people … It kills people on both ends, it's not just a [U.S. city] problem, it is an India problem too
Agile methodologies	Permeability of the border	Obviously, one of the things with SCRUM [an agile methodology] is … the interaction among your team-members … With a distributed team, one of the things I have seen done is to have SCRUM meetings in the morning and the evening. Again, this impacts work–life balance … "resistance" to SCRUM among GDSD developers, and a "preconceived notion that SCRUM was evil" perhaps due to being "always under pressure," the need to meet at odd times frequently, and because "the week before the end of the sprint … people were working 90-hour weeks just to catch up"
Supervisory support	Border keeper's support characteristics	I think [the manager] being more open with communication helps to keep the motivation and morale up … [Saying that] 'I know you guys had to work the weekend … and I know that sucks … [but] there is a light at the end of the tunnel, and I really do appreciate the work the team is doing … I think that would improve morale a lot if I have to take a 7 a.m. call and a 9 p.m. call … my manager's right there with me backing me up …
Family-friendly policies	Border keeper's support characteristics	We are all having an afternoon at the park. We are inviting families and so some of those things are planned for to help keep that morale up … We do morale outings from time to time, especially if we have occasions where [some members of] two or more of those specific geographic teams get together … be [it] a restaurant or some other fun miniature golf event
Task dependency	Reliance of border crosser on other domain members	… [for] anything and everything … they [located in India] have to ask me [located in the U.S.] a question, I can only do so much in a day. I can only work 16/17 h in a day … So I become the bottleneck … Everything [offshore] was dependent on me

(continued)

Table 2.1 (continued)

Variable suggested	*Category of the variable suggested by border theory*	*Sample quote*
Changing nature of requirements	Domain characteristics	The coordination required to pull [everyone] together and really achieve all these code changes on a short timeline was incredible...
Heterogeneity of technical platforms	Domain characteristics	You need to make sure that the 7 components are working together and integrates well ... Even today, we have bandwidth issues from India We have a policy that all source code will be [here in the U.S.] because of security, because we have backup systems here. [Because of the different infrastructures at the different locations], merging and making sure that the final end product [has] the right integrativity [capability to be integrated] is the biggest issue.

Specifically, researchers note that the degree of geographical dispersion can affect the level of difficulty for the border crosser in seamlessly transitioning between the borders (Clark, 2000). A number of researchers have examined virtual teams and networks on the basis of physical proximity or propinquity (Corman, 1990; Jablin & Putnam, 2000; Johnson, 1992). Extending this line of work on proximity of teams, O'Leary and Cummings (2007) argue that the high levels of physical dispersion lead to higher complexity in coordination, communication, and other forms of interaction. Such intense work-related coordination and communication demands pose additional strains on employees and force employees to compromise on their personal lives and family. Dealing with these competing demands entails juggling different priorities, creating friction among the work and family domains.

Researchers have found that when team members are required to interact with colleagues in multiple locations, the potential for complexity also increases (e.g., Sarker & Sahay, 2004). There are several likely contributing factors to this complexity. First, it is more difficult to develop cohesion if a team is not sharing the same space. The potential of having disparate goals is increased, creating a "significant burden" for staff members (Kishore et al., 2006). Second, cultural differences resulting from non-co-located members may require additional time for team members to build rapport and trust (Barcus & Montibeller, 2008).

Next, there is also the additional challenge of "expertise coordination," as team members may not be able to easily identify colleagues who are the experts for a given aspect of software development (Faraj & Sproull, 2000). Finally, a distributed team will also require the border crosser to frequently travel to other locations for coordination, adding to their WLC. A contractor in the United States shared the following:

> I would love being home every night and sleeping in my own bed and eating my own food and all that, but [have to travel] every week.

Thus, we have:

Hypothesis 1 (H1): *IT professionals involved in globally distributed settings that involve workers from across a larger number of sites will experience higher WLC than those IT professionals involved in globally distributed settings that do not involve workers from across a larger number of sites.*

Extent of Temporal Borders: Time Differences with Remote Members

Border Theory addresses the role of temporal borders, often manifested as time overlaps between the domains (Clark, 2000). In distributed teams, temporal separation among domains occurs when the individuals are separated by time zone differences with other coworkers (Carmel & Espinosa, 2011). While today's communication technologies enable distributed software development and other types of work to be conducted across time and place, it "often results in people working longer and at a faster pace" (Gambles et al., 2006, pp. 47–48). The difference in time zone leads to coordination challenges (Balaji & Ahuja, 2005), which means that at least one part of the global team has to compromise their sleep time (Espinosa et al., 2003). This, in turn, leads to increased WLC and can eventually lead to turnover in the long run. Our interviews provided evidence that WLB can be adversely affected when distributed work requires working across time zones. For example, differences in time zones, especially in cases where there is no (or limited) overlap of traditional working hours among team members, create challenges with scheduling meetings. One of our interviewees commented:

> Sometimes [there were meetings] early morning and late night... Team 1 in the morning, and Team 2 in the evening, right. It kills people... It kills people on both ends, it's not just a [U.S. city] problem, it is an India problem too.

A software production planner in Denmark reiterated how working in multiple time zones, especially in cases where working hours do not overlap, can be a major challenge as it relates to scheduling meetings. In his case, at least three times per week, he would participate in calls spanning three or four time zones. To accommodate the multiple time zones, these meetings would occur as early as 6:30 A.M. and extend into the late evening. Indeed, one of his coworkers told us about a call that ended at 3:30 A.M. Similarly, a female human resources team member in India involved in an offshoring arrangement also shared the need to be available in the late evenings, typically 7 or 8 P.M., for calls. In her case, these calls would typically relate to new human resource policies and related decisions. In India, a female product documentation designer found that meetings could go until 2:00 or 3:00 in the morning, with other calls starting as early as 5:00 in the morning.

The frequency of off-hours meetings seems to be a concern as it relates to WLC. A product manager in India experienced a significantly higher number of off-hours calls each week, as many as a dozen, but typically four to five calls each week. He shared:

> If you're an individual contributor, you don't conference that much. But you become a manager and you're responsible for certain things. Then you get pulled into all sorts of meetings and you need to make sure you're available.

A female engineering group member in India mentioned that she was routinely on early morning or late evening calls three to four times a week. She shared that these meetings were:

> pretty much a daily event. If it was once in a month, I probably wouldn't mind or once a two weeks...it wouldn't be a big deal, but...

Regularly scheduled collaborative design or troubleshooting meetings and conference calls for coordination during nonwork times can be inconvenient for some IT workers, many of whom experience "mismatches in the physiological and social rhythms" and work spillovers into personal or leisure time (Sarker & Sahay, 2004, p. 9). Over time, such spillovers can be detrimental to the well-being of the workers, leading them to experience greater work–life conflict. Thus, we have:

Hypothesis 2 (H2): *IT workers involved in globally distributed work with less work time overlap with remote colleagues will experience higher WLC than those with more work time overlap.*

Flexibility of Border and WLC

As discussed earlier, Border Theory argues that the flexibility of the border has a bearing on the extent to which border crossing occurs smoothly. Flexibility refers to the ease with which a border expands or contracts. The notion of flexibility of the border is related to the idea of workplace flexibility (Kossek et al., 2004) and is informed by past scholarship on WLC. Kossek et al. (2004) refer to this type of flexibility as "personal job flexibility autonomy" and as the availability of flextime and autonomy over one's schedule. Others have defined it as "the ability of workers to make choices influencing when, where, and for how long they engage in work-related tasks" (Hill et al., 2008, p. 152). Richman et al. (2008, p. 186) argue that flexibility improves the fit between work and life domains by enhancing their "ability to meet demands of roles in each domain."

Flexibility is quite prevalent in IT work, especially for those in distributed settings. A male engineering manager in India found that senior staff:

> are required to basically work in this kind of arrangement where they can be flexible in coming late and … can stay late here.

Alternatively, some choose to work from home, thereby experiencing flexibility of the location. A senior software engineer in the United States felt that:

> working in a distributed environment actually creates a good deal of freedom… It's common for people to have laptops that they can take home with them. So, you can do work from home, or you can do work from work. And since the work is distributed, it's not so much required to do it in the office, and since it is distributed and we're expected to be present at multiple, various times, most managers in the company have an attitude

> for - at least for engineering... The basic attitude is, 'I don't care when you get your work done, as long as you get your work done.' So, if you need to go to the doctor, you go to the doctor. You just take care of your work elsewhere or at a different time. If you have, say, something to do with your kids that's important and it doesn't conflict with any of the other high priorities, like being at a meeting, then you take care of it. And many, many engineers will do this... because we have a distributed environment, we're not tied to the office as much as other people.

Contrary to popular views, Clark (2000) suggests that high flexibility of borders makes them weak, creating expansive *borderlands* in which employees find it difficult to juggle different demands from the two sides of the border. Extending this idea to the notion of flextime and flexibility of work schedules, Clark (2000, p. 758) specifically argues that flextime often leaves employees more frustrated since they find it difficult to negotiate with *both* family and employers in terms of where "work and home responsibilities are carried out." We see a similar sentiment echoed by some of the IT professionals we interviewed. For example, an engineering manager from India highlighted:

> if you're talking about work-life balance, if you're taking a call from home also, you're not productive [dedicated] at home, in that sense.

Another example of this comes from a male software engineer in the United States who told us about receiving a call that he felt that he needed to take, while he was out at a movie theater with his wife. This expectation of being available "didn't go over so well with my wife, or myself," he felt. Thus, we have:

Hypothesis 3 (H3): *IT professionals involved in globally distributed settings where they have flexible work schedules will experience higher WLC than those with less flexible work schedules.*

Permeability of the Border

Similar to flexibility, permeability also causes spillovers from the work to the life domain (Clark, 2000). While flexibility of a border is associated with how easy the border between domains might shift, permeability relates to the amount of stress from one domain that might enter another domain (Sarker et al., 2018). When work-related activities spillover to family time, it can cause blurring of the boundaries (Clark, 2000). In the context of this study, this is likely to happen when the individuals working in globally distributed settings use agile methodologies such as SCRUM (an agile methodology which requires close, ongoing interaction, including daily meetings, between team members to ensure that projects are moving forward in a rapid, coordinated manner). Such meetings in a distributed environment, owing to the time differences, are likely to be held at times that repeatedly cause spillovers into the family domain.

Earlier studies have suggested that agile practices, such as an open culture with expectations of close communication, are accompanied by higher levels of stress, especially when situated in a global development context (Fowler, 2003). Short timelines, also a factor in agile methodologies, can create WLB challenges. A technical lead in India noted that the heaviest times are when new versions of the software are being released. At other times, the focus is more on product maintenance and qualifying new projects. In Denmark, a software production planner found that pressures to meet deadlines, especially in operationally oriented coding work, required intense, sometimes 24-hour, workdays to complete the error fixing, correction, and debugging required prior to the deadline. His perception was:

> ...during those periods, there is no such thing as work-life balance for certain people involved in certain tasks.

An engineering group manager in India found that given the high pace of agile approaches, and to meet sprint deadlines, project teams were often asked to work on Saturdays, spilling over to family time. She was grateful this did not happen to her team. Her perception was that the managers:

> ...probably didn't manage it right, alright? If you are asking people to work over the evenings and over the weekends, you're probably not accounting for the time well enough... So that was more in [about] how well you manage the project, and you didn't manage it well.

The second relates to the role, such as testers who needed to be available on short notice in agile projects. A senior technical lead in India, earlier in his career, had spent time as a tester. In this role, he would work regular hours during the day and conduct testing concurrently with

US offices overnight. At least once a week, he would be at work for 24 to 36 hours straight. Working excessive hours was not unusual. A female product documentation designer in India shared:

> I did once a cycle where we were working 18 hours a day. And for three months, we were on an 18-hour cycle. At the end of it, we said that we are quitting or you've got to improve things for us. They said okay, we'll try and change things.

Other aspects of agile, fueled by this ongoing communication, include development cycles that are short and iterative, decision-making in a collaborative format, and the expectation of rapid implementation of changes (Nerur et al., 2005), can all also raise the level of WLC. Thus, we have:

Hypothesis 4 (H4): *IT professionals involved in globally distributed work using agile methodologies will experience higher WLC than those who are not using agile methodologies.*

The Role of the Border Keepers: Supervisory Support, Organizational Policies, and WLC

Supervisors and the organizational policies/procedures regarding employee well-being are considered to be the primary border keepers within the work domain and play a significant role in managing WLC. Clark (2000) argues that frequent engagement with supportive border keepers helps border crossers deal with the imbalance. Consistent with this argument, a number of studies suggest that having a supportive supervisor can help reduce one's WLC (e.g., Allen, 2001). Similarly, family friendly policies (FFPs) (Felstead et al., 2002) implemented by organizations have been found to reduce WLC. Such policies may include features such as on-site day care, on-site elder care, and help with access to care. Both a supportive supervisor and FFPs signify that the organization "is sensitive to employees' family needs and doesn't demand the prioritization of work over family" (Jang, 2009, p. 94). Thus, we have:

Hypothesis 5 (H5): *IT workers involved in GDSD who have supportive supervisors will experience lower WLC than those without supportive supervisors.*

Hypothesis 6 (H6): *IT workers involved in GDSD who work in organizations with FFPs will experience lower WLC than those with fewer FFP.*

Border Crossers' Dependency on Members Across Borders: Task Dependency and WLC

The level of reliance a border crosser has on other domain members has been shown to play a role in WLB (Clark, 2000). Our qualitative interviews suggest that this level of reliance can arise due to the nature of task interdependency. Task interdependency is defined as the "degree to which group members must rely on one another to perform their tasks effectively" (Saavedra et al., 1993, p. 61). Task interdependence may be pooled (members contribute without much interaction), sequential (one member finishes a task before another member starts), reciprocal (one member's output becomes the other member's input or vice versa), or interdependent (where members jointly work on the task at hand with high levels of collaboration, often undertaking problem-solving together) (Thompson, 1967). We found that individuals who felt another distributed location relied on them to complete a task felt stretched and always under pressure to get work done on time so as to not cause project delays. Often, coding and design work has a similar form of dependency and require a great deal of planning, working under time pressure, and coordination. A supply chain manager in Denmark suggested that dependencies in the work are very difficult to manage and will often lead to at least one team member needing to stay up all night at some point during the project:

> …let's say there are some amount of code needs to be written and some pieces of that code are dependent on other pieces of code..produce[d] by other teams that are sitting somewhere else, I think it can still be managed but it just needs a lot of planning and coordination. And the end result is that nobody can really plan and coordinate like that and, therefore, you often get into situations where somebody will be forced to sit up overnight and finish something.

Whether someone is causing the bottleneck or waiting for a decision, the result is the same: stress and consequently increased WLC. A senior developer recognized that he had become the bottleneck:

> [for] anything and everything ...they have to ask me a question, I can only do some much in a day. I can only work 16/17 hours in a day... So I become the bottleneck... Everything [offshore] was dependent on me.

In some cases, meetings must occur during off-hours. A senior software engineer in the United States found that dependency in his work required him to plan team meetings with colleagues in different parts of the world. In his words:

> ...occasionally, I'll have to take an evening phone call or have a phone call that would come at my usual dinner hour... And so, I'll have to offset my eating a little bit. Occasionally, I'll have to start my workday at say, midnight and go until eight in the morning. You know, dependent upon - because I interact with people.

To summarize, the level of dependency that employees have on other domain members can cause strains related to workload balancing, inability to plan work time, and uncertainty regarding task outcomes—which can all lead to WLC. For example, Dierdoff and Ellington (2008) argue that increased dependence results in frequent "boundary-spanning" activities for the individual. Such boundary-spanning activities significantly reduce the strength of the border and tend to raise the level of WLC (Greenhaus & Beutell, 1985). Thus, we have:

Hypothesis 7 (H7): *IT workers involved in globally distributed work with greater task interdependence across distributed locations will experience higher WLC than those with less task interdependence across distributed locations.*

Effect of the Domain Characteristics: Nature of the Software Requirements, Technology Platforms, and WLC

Our qualitative interviews also highlighted that, in the context of IT work such as software or application development, the nature of the software requirements influenced the level of WLC. One of the core characteristics of distributed software development projects is that they often influence project stakeholders' stress and performance due to *uncertainty of the requirements* (e.g., Nidumolu, 1995). This is because software development is often an iterative process, during which the client may change their requirements as the project evolves. Research suggests that the primary aspects of requirements uncertainty are requirements instability, defined as the "the extent of changes in user requirements," and requirements diversity, defined as the "the extent to which users differ among themselves in their requirements" (Nidumolu, 1996, p. 136). In fact, many globally distributed project managers and developers, with remote clients (sometimes distributed across multiple locations), find themselves being heavily involved in interpreting the meaning of the requirements, which are often fluid and unclear, given the variety of perspectives held by different stakeholders embedded in distributed contexts (e.g., Sarker & Sarker, 2009). Uncertainty in the requirements can lead to higher conflict among the users and the analysts (Nidumolu, 1995), and IT professionals are likely to find themselves spending additional time in understanding the requirements and coordinating across the distributed locations to ensure that all relevant team members share that understanding, thereby raising their WLC levels.

Disagreements about any of these aspects may lead to conflict (Nidumolu, 1995), requiring the offshore worker to invest time meeting with different stakeholder groups to clarify objectives and reduce conflicts. These additional meetings often impact personal time, leading to reduced WLB (Sarker et al., 2018). Thus, we argue:

Hypothesis 8 (H8): *IT professionals involved in globally distributed work with unstable requirements will experience higher WLC than those who work with more stable requirements.*

Hypothesis 9 (H9): *IT professionals involved in globally distributed projects with diverse requirements will experience higher WLC than those with more homogenous requirements.*

Technology Diversity

Consistent with the difficulties described by some of our interviewees, Xia and Lee (2005) indicate that the need for coordination increases with the multiplicity and interdependence of a project's technology platforms and software environments. In addition, Lee et al. (2006) highlight the significant challenges that can arise within globally distributed teams when members are not working on a similar technological platform. Also, in distributed projects, a greater diversity of data formats for exporting data to, and importing data from, other systems exists, increasing the likelihood of errors in the code (Schmidt et al., 2001). Finally, the likelihood of different team members using different hardware or software platforms for the same task increases as the team's level of distribution increases. Therefore, there is an additional level of strain in attempting to translate between technology platforms (e.g., Oshri et al., 2009). Thus, we have:

Hypothesis 10 (H10): *IT workers involved in globally distributed projects where there is a greater variety of technological platforms/infrastructures will experience higher WLC than those with a lower variety of technological platforms/infrastructures.*

Methods

Included in this chapter is a brief overview of the methods. Please see Appendix 3 for a more elaborate explanation of the methods used in our study. In testing our model, we employed a survey of IT professionals involved in globally distributed work from the United States, United Kingdom, and India. The United States was chosen because it is the main country of interest for the researchers and engages in a significant amount of distributed software development with other countries. The United Kingdom serves as the IT hub for distributed software development in Europe, and India provides a significant proportion of IT workers for GDSD projects (Robinson & Kalakota, 2004). Further, for this particular chapter, we subscribe to the "convergence" perspective (Stohl, 2001), which argues for the absence of across country differences in the new industrialized economy. Our primary motive for surveying subjects from three different countries was to ensure that we did not inadvertently introduce bias associated with perspectives from one country only.

Perceptions about WLC may be influenced based on the individual's country. Thus, in an effort to remain open to possible differences that could emerge, the country was included as a control variable. We coded respondents as 1, 2, or 3 depending on whether they came from India, United Kingdom, and United States.

We also controlled for *gender* and whether *individuals take care of dependents* or not. Such variables have been chosen to be control variables for studies related to WLC (e.g., Dierdoff & Ellington, 2008; Lambert et al., 2004). We measured each of these with single items.

Further, since prior experience in working in distributed software development can be drawn on in addressing the challenges of distribution, we also sought to control for participants' *prior experience in globally distributed settings*. Indeed, from our interviews, it appeared that employees with experience in the distributed environment had organized their life *accepting and accommodating the incursions of work, while setting aside times for personal and family life*. Finally, we controlled for the *role* they played in their organization. Specifically, we asked respondents to specify their roles from a given set of options, which we coded as having primarily technical or a primarily project management/relationship management role.

Among our sample of 1000 GDSD participants, 500 were from the United States, 251 from the United Kingdom, and 249 from India. Regarding gender, 767 were males, and 233 were females. Related to roles, 345 played a project management-related role, while 655 were in more technical roles. Their average experience in distributed software development was 6.59 years, and a median experience of 5 years. As far as caring for dependents, 498 of the respondents indicated that they needed to take care of dependents, while 502 did not.

Where possible, we used established measures such as Kopelman et al. (1983) eight items for measuring WLC. *Supervisory support* was assessed using an adapted version of Thomas and Ganster's (1995) nine items plus two additional items validated in a prior study involving a sample of IT professionals from India (Sarker et al., 2010). Nine items adapted from prior research, namely, the Perceived Organizational Family Support (POFS) scale, which captures perceptions of tangible and intangible support provided by an organization (Jahn et al., 2003; Thompson et al., 2004), were used for assessing the role of *Organizational FFPs*. *Flexible work arrangements* was measured using four items adapted from Greenhaus et al. (1989).

Nidumolu's (1995, 1996) items were used for measuring aspects of *requirements uncertainty*. Specifically, four items for measuring requirements instability, and three items for measuring requirements diversity in their projects were used. The use of *agile methodologies* in the project was assessed by the following two items: On a scale of 1 (Always) to 7 (Rarely), indicates the extent to which agile methodologies (such as SCRUM) were used in their globally distributed projects, and (2) the extent to which agile development principles was used in their distributed IT projects.

Respondents were asked to provide the largest *time difference* they had with their remote colleagues. From this information, a categorical variable was created that captured the time difference with remote colleagues (e.g., 9–12 hours was coded as 3, time difference of 4–8 hours as 2, and a time difference of 3 or less hours was coded as 1). *Technology diversity* was assessed using an item that asked for the number of different technical platforms on which the team members worked. *Extent of physical borders (or locational dispersion)* was measured using one item that asked respondents to specify on average, the number of countries in which their team members were located. Finally, *task interdependence* was measured using three items on a scale of 1 (disagree) to 7 (agree): (1) Tasks your distributed team members performed were related to tasks that you performed, (2) you could accomplish your tasks without information or materials from your distributed team members, and (3) your distributed team members depend on you for information or materials to complete their work.

Findings from the Survey

Before we present the specific results, it is important to reiterate the importance of focusing on the antecedents of WLC. One of the primary reasons is that by understanding the antecedents, organizations can actively work toward reducing WLC for their employees, especially since it has shown to have detrimental effects on several outcome variables. Much of the WLB/WLC literature has drawn attention to the idea of relational *exchanges*, which highlights that when an employee views "the employer as supportive," he/she "is likely to return the gesture" through positive attitudes such as lower turnover intentions (Cropanzano & Mitchell, 2005, p. 883). However, feelings of an inequitable exchange between the employee and the organization, in the form of work practices that lead to high WLC, can lead to employees perceiving "their organizations as unsupportive" and attempting to leave the organization (Aryee et al., 2005, p. 135). In a study of IT workers, Ahuja et al. (2007) found that work overload and work–family conflict affected turnover intentions. Similarly, the negative effect of WLC on the productivity of employees has also been suggested in the literature not related to IT professionals (e.g.,

Felstead et al., 2002; Netemeyer et al., 2004). Employees who experience WLC are likely to be continuously stressed, owing to their inability to balance the demands of their family and their work, and this can lead to unfavorable outcomes. Thus, before testing our model, we examined the effect of WLC on the outcome variables of *turnover intention* and *performance*. Turnover intention was measured using four items adapted from Mitchell et al. (2001). Performance was measured using two items adapted from Dubinsky and Mattson (1979). Results indicated a strong positive effect of WLC on turnover intentions (.395, $p < .01$) but an insignificant effect of WLC on performance (−.023, $p > .10$). We revisit this part about the effect of WLC on performance and turnover intention in Chapter 3.

We used SmartPLS 2.0 M3 to analyze our survey data. Consistent with prior research using PLS models, we analyzed our model in two stages (e.g., Bhattacherjee & Premkumar, 2004; Chin, 1998; Gefen & Straub, 2005; Hulland, 1999): The first stage involved "the assessment of the reliability and the validity of the measurement model," and the second stage involved "the assessment of the structural model" (Hulland, 1999, p. 198).

Assessment of the Hypothesized Relationships: In the analysis, we controlled for gender, care for dependents, and experience in distributed software development while assessing the models. As suggested in prior research (e.g., Kock, 2011), in PLS, control variables are included as independent variables as part of the study without hypothesizing for its effect. Finally, we first tested the models (and the hypotheses) using the entire sample. Our results indicated that our hypotheses were mostly supported. The role of flexibility was significant, contributing to increased WLC, not reduced WLC that many might expect. The role of the use of agile methods and technology diversity on WLC was weakly supported. Among the control variables, care for dependents had a significant effect on work–life conflict with individuals who need to take care of dependents experiencing more conflict. Table 2.2 summarizes the results.

Hypotheses 1 and 2 suggested that increased locational and temporal dispersion would lead to higher levels of WLC. Both hypotheses were supported, indicating that employees who work with individuals in different locations, and especially those where time zones do not overlap, will likely experience higher levels of WLC.

Hypotheses 3 and 4 relate to flexibility and permeability of the border between work and life activities. Hypothesis 3 was supported. The results

Table 2.2 Findings from hypothesis testing

Hypothesis #	*Independent variable*	*Dependent Variable*	*Nature of Result* (β; *significance level)*
N/A	Gender (control variable)	WLC	.026; ns
N/A	Family Structure (control variable)		−.099; p < .01
N/A	Experience in GDSD (control variable)		−.019; ns
N/A	Role (control variable)		.111; p < .01
N/A	Country (control variable)		−.005; ns
H1	Locational Dispersion		.069; p < .05; Supported
H2	Temporal Dispersion		.056; p < .05; Supported
H3	Flex_Schedule		.086; p < .05; Supported
H4	Agile_methods_Use		−.058; p < .10; Marginally Supported
H5	Supervisory_Support		−.118; p < .01; Supported
H6	Organizational FFPs		−.141; p < .01; Supported
H7	Task_Dependency		.082; p < .01; Supported
H8	Requirements Instability		.101; p < .01; Supported
H9	Requirements_Diversity		.187; p < .01; Supported
H10	Technology_Diversity		.054; p < .10; Marginally Supported

are consistent with the recent arguments by Beauregard and Henry (2009), that the effect of flexibility on WLC is contextual and is especially meaningful where individuals have high demands for dependent care or prefer segmentation of work and life. In the context of globally distributed IT settings, where work tends to be carried out around the clock, a flexible schedule often means that employees need to be available for questions/clarifications and for dealing with urgent situations around the clock (e.g., Sarker & Sahay, 2004), which would understandably lead to higher rather than lower WLC.

Hypothesis 4, which proposed that the use of agile methodologies would correspond with higher levels of WLC among workers, was only marginally supported. The effect of the use of agile methods and principles, which is an important facet of understanding Information Systems Development (ISD) (Tripp et al., 2016), also received marginal support. The lack of strong support could probably be understood by considering that (1) while agile methods were being used by many of our survey participants (about 350/1,000 survey respondents indicated using agile principles "Always" to "Often"), the fact that these approaches were not used by a large proportion could have affected the results; and (2) an intriguing study by Desrochers et al. (2005) that argued that when it comes to work–life conflict, it is the permeability of the "home" border that has more of an effect than the permeability of the "work" border. In our study, in examining the impact of agile approaches, our focus has been on the *work border*, and the weak effect of permeability on work–life conflict could have resulted from this focus. Given that this study is the first known empirical test of the permeability of a border in the context of IT professionals, it represents an important first step. However, more studies need to be conducted, distinguishing between home border and work border, before the effect of the permeability in this context can be understood with greater certainty.

Hypotheses 5 and 6, which proposed that companies with supportive supervisors and FFPs would correspond with lower levels of WLC, were both supported by the data collected in the survey. The final three hypotheses related to software requirements and technology platforms. Hypotheses 8 and 9 were both supported by the data, indicating that both unstable requirements and diverse requirements are associated with higher levels of WLC among workers. Hypothesis 10 suggested that when IT personnel work with distributed members using different sets of technology platforms, it can lead to high work–life conflict for them. Our results supported this hypothesis only marginally. One of the reasons for this could be the fact that the current IT professional, just like other individuals around the world, is used to the multiplicity of technologies and devices in their daily lives, and thus shifting between platforms may not be a cause of concern anymore. Another reason could be that in the software industry, there is generally a push toward uniformity as well as interoperability of platforms. For example, Meyer and Seliger (1998) suggest that companies such as Microsoft have moved toward the creation of robust platforms over which a myriad of software applications can be developed.

Implications and Conclusion

In this chapter, we have provided an overview of various aspects of IT workers work domain that may adversely affect WLB. The results highlight that ideally, to reduce individual workers' WLC, organizations should: (1) attempt to design teams with fewer distributed locations and with minimal time-zone differences, (2) not assume that offering greater flexibility of work schedules is necessarily desirable, (3) be cautious about the use of agile methodologies in distributed contexts, (4) have a supportive supervisor and generous organizational FFPs, and (5) carefully manage requirements uncertainty and diversity, and greater variance in the technology platforms in projects. The results specifically highlight that while WLC is an issue in most organizations, irrespective of the nature of tasks undertaken by employees, the globally distributed IT context or the GDSD context adds layers of challenges arising from the time and space distances and the unique characteristics of IT work such as software development. Our study suggests that a certain level of WLC in this context is unavoidable, and it is often challenging to satisfy the guidelines (mentioned above) for reducing an IT workers' WLC. Nevertheless, firms engaged in distributed work need to continue to look for creative ways of managing the WLC of their employees. Following are some practical guidelines to that effect. Before discussing the implications, we recall that even though we do not focus on this result in this chapter, in our study, we found WLC to be significantly and positively related to turnover intention. However, we did not find a significant relationship between WLC and performance. Here are some guidelines that emerge from the study.

Guideline #1: Related to Locational and Temporal Dispersion

Temporal and geographical/locational dispersion can both be challenging for WLC. In the short term, it may be difficult to adjust the time differences among collaborative sites and the distances between locations. That said, our interviews suggested several tactics to address this challenge, including working with individual staff schedules to identify optimal times for meetings, sharing the burden between worksites related to meeting times, and scheduling work around meetings. For example, a program manager in Denmark found that 5 P.M. local time was the optimal time for meetings, as it was 8 A.M. at the company's headquarters.

A contractor in the United States offered an interesting perspective related to an arrangement to accommodate workers in other parts of the world

> When you try to accommodate everyone, we accommodated no one. So, we... made the sacrifice to work from 12:00 A.M. to 2:00 A.M. to accommodate Australia and 6:00 A.M. to 8:00 A.M. for the U.K.

In another case, employees agreed to share the stress of off-hours calls. Specifically, coworkers negotiated and alternated who would be participating at off-hours. Mentally feeling that "I'm not the only one who is stretching every time or every night or every week..." seemed to make it easier.

Where there is time overlap in working hours, work can often be arranged around meetings. A design manager in India mentioned having coworkers in Spain. His team planned on working on internal tasks the first half of the day, leaving time available in the afternoons for meetings and interaction with staff members in the Spanish office.

Guideline #2: Related to Flexibility and Permeability of the Border

One of our interviews suggested that when companies are open to negotiating availability, employees may be more willing to compromise. An engineering group manager in India found that distributed work comes with an expectation of always being available, specifically, "they think they can call you at any time and ask you to get work done." For the most part, she was able to manage the interruptions, although she also mentioned that she recently had to say "no" to a request to be available.

Too much flexibility can also make it difficult to manage a project. A design manager in India found that flexible scheduling for staff posed challenges in managing the day-to-day work of the organization, especially as it related to scheduling meetings and completing work that was reliant on other people to complete. In his case, he chose to ask his staff to transition back to a regular work schedule. In his words::

> ...even though they are coming in a little early, we have a lot of time in the evening to spend with our families. So, things fall in the right perspective.

Planning is another strategy that interviewees felt should be managed better. In the eyes of a senior technical lead in India, appeals to work late or work weekends was not due, necessarily, to working within a distributed environment. Rather:

> ...it has always been about a lack of planning, not about distributed things because the distributed environment, people who might face problems are...as we said, they don't want to work on those overlap times or due to family constraints they can't work, otherwise there shouldn't be any issues.

Poor planning may also lead to panic responses, which were often not productive. Indeed, a technical lead in India suggested that stressful situations related to software development can lead to team members being driven by panic and reacting to situations rather than being deliberate and following a well thought out plan. He provided the following reflection:

> ...suppose I'm driving back home and I got a call. 'So, this is [not working], how did this happen?' And either I have to come back or I have to go home... [and] log in. ...by end of the time, I came and see it is a very silly issue. It is not required to panic that much. So, instead of me panicking and thinking in a bigger way, try to be resolved within ourself, take it, make it cool, but that is not happening. Maybe that is because of who are the managers are leading that particular project, they may not be having in that. ... So, all this, how it is and now, we are reacting over the things. Instead of reaction mechanism, we can predict on, we can try to react on character things, I feel it is much better.

Engaging in regular and consistent planning can help to avoid WLC challenges.

Guidance #3: Related to Supervisory Support and Organizational Policies

In the interviews, some suggestions for managers emerged. These are related to communication and information sharing, culture building, offering flexible hours, scheduling, and being sensitive to their staff members' needs. The participants also had some suggestions for the organization. These included considerations such as flexibility in scheduling meetings, having WLB-friendly human resource policies, offering job flexibility, and ensuring adequate planning for projects. We note that our empirical result showed that *schedule flexibility* of a worker isn't necessarily beneficial from the WLC perspective.

Guideline #4: Related to Task Interdependence and the Need to Schedule Overlapping Times Across Locations

In distributed settings, modularized work that is less dependent on others, especially across geographically and temporally distant locations, can be helpful. A senior technical lead in India found that individual contributors, whose work does not immediately need to be integrated with other pieces, often experienced less WLC. We will see much more on this theme in Chapter 4 where we present a case study of offshore insourcing. However, when others in the office are dependent on their work, having regularly scheduled work hours is helpful. In the office this technical lead worked in, they chose specific times when everyone would be in the office so that they could all be available for synchronous communication:

> I think most of the companies manage – I will not say all… when they say flexible hours, they don't mean you can come night nine to morning six or afternoon… whenever you can come. They usually say that, 'Okay, to begin, part-time of the office does not show up at nine, it may not be ten, it may not be eleven, but be present in the office from eleven to four or eleven to three.' There should be some overlap for us, so that if we are scheduling any meetings or any trainings, it can be scheduled in those times and around that you can plan your time… Not exactly flexible hours, but providing still some flexibility.

Guideline #5: Related to the Nature of Software Requirements and Technology Platforms

WLC can also be managed by keeping in mind the nature of the IT project being undertaken. For instance, projects with low levels of requirements instability and diversity (e.g., a routine maintenance project) may have a lower need for active management of WLC, in comparison to one that has high levels of requirements instability and diversity.

Building on research in the context of GDSD, this chapter outlined factors that contribute to a distributed knowledge worker's WLC. These factors were nested in the framework suggested by Border Theory, and include considerations such as geographical and temporal distance, flexibility of schedules, supervisory support, FFPs, the systems methodology used (such as agile approaches), the nature of requirements, and the nature of IT infrastructure or platforms. We believe that the results of our study can help guide managers involved in designing structures and processes of distributed teams undertaking IT-related and other knowledge work. In the next chapter, we focus on the effect of individual-level factors pertaining to the border crosser on WLC.

References

Ahuja, M. K., Chudoba, K. M., Kacmar, C. J., McKnight, D. H., & George, J. F. (2007). IT road warriors: Balancing work-family conflict, job autonomy, and work overload to mitigate turnover intentions. *MIS Quarterly, 31*(1), 1–17.

Allen, T. D. (2001). Family-supportive work environments: The role of organizational perceptions. *Journal of Vocational Behavior, 58*(3), 414–435.

Aryee, S., Srinivas, E. S., & Tan, H. H. (2005). Rhythms of life: Antecedents and outcomes of work-family balance in employed parents. *Journal of Applied Psychology, 90*(1), 132–146.

Balaji, S., & Ahuja, M. K. (2005). Critical team-level success factors of offshore outsourced projects: A knowledge integration perspective. In *Proceedings of 38th Annual Hawaii International Conference* (pp. 52–59). IEEE.

Barcus, A., & Montibeller, G. (2008). Supporting the allocation of software development work in distributed teams with multi-criteria decision analysis. *Omega, 36*(3), 464–475.

Beauregard, T. A., & Henry, L. C. (2009). Making the link between worklife balance practices and organizational performance. *Human Resource Management Review, 19*(1), 9–22.

Bhattacherjee, A., & Premkumar, G. (2004). Understanding changes in belief and attitude toward information technology usage: A theoretical model and longitudinal test. *MIS Quarterly, 28*(2), 229–254.

Carmel, E., & Espinosa, J. A. (2011). *I'm working while they're sleeping: Time zone separation challenges and solutions.* Nedder Stream Press.

Chin, W. W. (1998). Issues and opinion on structural equation modeling. *MIS Quarterly, 22*(1), vii–xvi.

Clark, S. C. (2000). Work/family border theory: A new theory of work/family balance. *Human Relations, 53*(6), 747–770.

Corman, S. R. (1990). A model of perceived communication in collective networks. *Human Communication Research, 16*(4), 582–602.

Cropanzano, R., & Mitchell, M. S. (2005). Social exchange theory: An interdisciplinary review. *Journal of Management, 31*(6), 874–900.

Desrochers, S., Hilton, J. M., & Larwood, L. (2005). Preliminary validation of the work-family integration-blurring scale. *Journal of Family Issues, 26*(4), 442–466.

Dierdoff, E. C., & Ellington, J. K. (2008). It's the nature of the work: Examining behavior-based sources of work-family conflict across occupations. *Journal of Applied Psychology, 93*(4), 883–892.

Dubinsky, A. J., & Mattson, B. E. (1979). Consequences of role conflict and ambiguity experienced by retail salespeople. *Journal of Retailing, 55*(Winter), 70–86.

Espinosa, J. A., Cummings, J. N., Wilson, J. M., & Pearce, B. M. (2003). Team boundary issues across multiple global firms. *Journal of Management Information Systems, 19*(4), 157–190.

Faraj, S., & Sproull, L. (2000). Coordinating expertise in software development teams. *Management Science, 46*(12), 1554–1568.

Felstead, A., Jewson, N., Phizacklea, A., & Walters, S. (2002). Opportunities to work at home in the context of work-life balance. *Human Resource Management Journal, 12*(1), 54–76.

Fowler, M. (2003). Using an agile software process with offshore development. *Capturado em.* http://martinfowler.com/articles/agileOffshore.html.

Gambles, R., Lewis, S., & Rapoport, R. (2006). *The myth of work-life balance: The challenge of our time for men, women, and societies.* Wiley.

Gefen, D., & Straub, D. W. (2005). A practical guide to factorial validity using PLS-graph: Tutorial and annotated example. *Communications of the Association for Information Systems, 16*(1), 91–109.

Greenhaus, J. H., & Beutell, N. J. (1985). Sources of conflict between work and family roles. *Academy of Management Review, 10*(1), 76–88.

Greenhaus, J. H., Parasuraman, S., Granrose, C. S., Rabinowitz, S., & Beutell, N. J. (1989). Sources of work-family conflict among two-career couples. *Journal of Vocational Behavior, 34*(2), 133–153.

Hill, E. J., Jacob, J. I., Shannon, L., Brennan, R. T., Blanchard, V. L., & Martinengo, G. (2008). Exploring the relationship of workplace flexibility, gender, and life stage to family-to-work conflict, and stress and burnout. *Community Work Family, 11*(2), 165–181.

Hulland, J. (1999). Use of partial least squares (PLS) in strategic management research: A review of four recent studies. Strategic *Management Journal, 20*(2), 195–204.

Jablin, F. M., & Putnam, L. L. (2000). *The new handbook of organizational communication: Advances in theory, research, and methods.* Sage.

Jahn, E. W., Thompson, C. A., & Kopelman R. E. (2003). Rationale and construct validity evidence for a measure of perceived organizational family support (POFS): Because purported practices may not reflect reality. *Community Work Family, 6*(2), 123–140.

Jang, S. J. (2009). The relationships of flexible work schedules, workplace support, supervisory support, work-life balance, and the well-being of working parents. *Journal of Social Service Research, 35*(2), 93–104.

Johnson, S. D. (1992). A framework for technology education curricula which emphasizes intellectual processes. *Journal of Technology Education, 3*(2), 29–40.

Kishore, R., Zhang, H., & Ramesh, R. (2006). Enterprise integration using the agent paradigm: Foundations of multi-agent-based integrative business information systems. *Decision support systems, 42*(1), 48–78.

Kock, N. (2011). Using WarpPLS in e-collaboration studies: Mediating effects, control and second order variables, and algorithm choices. International *Journal of e-Collaboration, 7*(3), 1–13.

Kopelman, R. E., Greenhaus, J. H., & Connelly, T. E. (1983). A model of work, family, and interrole conflict: A construct validation study. *Organizational Behavior and Human Performance, 32,* 198–215.

Kossek, E. E., Lautsch, B. A., & Eaton, S. C. (2004). Flexibility enactment theory: Implications of flexibility type, control, and boundary management for work-family effectiveness. In E. E. Kossek & S. J. Lambert (Eds.), *Work and life integration: Organizational, cultural, and individual perspectives* (pp. 243–261). Lawrence Erlbaum Associates.

Lambert, J., Agostoni, C., Elmadfa, I., Hulsof, K., Drause, E., Livingstone, B., et al. (2004). Dietary intake and nutritional status of children and adolescents in Europe. *British Journal of Nutrition, 92*(2), 147–211.

Lee, O. K. D., Banerjee, P., Lim, K. H., Kumar, K., Hillegersberg, J. V., & Wei, K. K. (2006). Aligning IT components to achieve agility in globally distributed system development. *Communications of the ACM, 49*(10), 49–54.

Meyer, M. H., & Seliger, R. (1998). Product platforms in software development. *MIT Sloan Management Review, 40*(1), 61–74.

Mitchell, T. R., Holtom, B. C., Lee, T. W., Sablynski, C. J., & Erez, M. (2001). Why people stay: Using job embeddedness to predict voluntary turnover. *Academy of Management Journal, 44*(6), 1102–1121.

Nerur, S., Mahapatra, R., & Mangalaraj, G. (2005). Challenges of migrating to agile methodologies. *Communications of the ACM, 48*(5), 72–78.

Netemeyer, R. G., Brashear-Alejandro, T., & Boles, J. S. (2004). A cross-national model of job-related outcomes of work role and family role variables: A retail sales context. *Academy of Marketing Science, 32*(1), 49–60.

Nidumolu, S. R. (1995). The effect of coordination and uncertainty on software project performance: Residual performance risk as an intervening variable. *Information Systems Research, 6*(3), 191–219.

Nidumolu, S. R. (1996). Standardization, requirements uncertainty, and software project performance. *Information & Management, 31*(3), 135–150.

O'Leary, M., & Cummings, J. N. (2007). The spatial, temporal, and configurational characteristics of geographic dispersion in work teams. *MIS Quarterly, 31*(3), 433–452.

Oshri, I., Kotlarsky, J., & Willcoks, L. P. (2009). *The handbook of global outsourcing and offshoring*. Macmillan.

Richman, A. L., Civian, J. T., Shannon, L. L., Hill, E. J., & Brennan, R. T. (2008). The relationship of perceived flexibility to employee engagement and expected retention. *Community Work Family, 11*(2), 183–197.

Riemenschneider, C. K., & Armstrong, D. J. (forthcoming). The development of the perceived distinctiveness antecedent of information systems professional identity. *Management Information Systems Quarterly*.

Robinson, M., & Kalakota, R. (2004). *Offshore outsourcing: Business models, ROI and best practices*. Alpharetta, GA: Mivar Press.

Saavedra, R., Early, P., & Van Dyne, L. (1993). Complex interdependence in task-performing groups. *Journal of Applied Psychology, 78*(1), 61–72.

Sarker, S., Ahuja, M., & Sarker, S. (2018). Work–life conflict of globally distributed software development personnel: An empirical investigation using border theory. *Information Systems Research, 29*(1), 103–126.

Sarker, S., & Sahay, S. (2004). Implications of space and time for distributed work: An interpretive study of Norwegian systems development teams. *European Journal of Information Systems, 13*(1), 3–20.

Sarker, S., Sarker, S., & Jana, D. (2010). The impact of the nature of globally distributed work arrangement on WLC and valence. *European Journal of Information Systems, 19*(2), 209–222.

Sarker, S., & Sarker, S. (2009). Exploring agility in distributed information systems development teams: An interpretive study in an offshoring context. *Information Systems Research, 20*(3), 440–461.

Schmidt, H., Poernomo, I., & Reussner, R. (2001). Trust-by-contract: Modelling, analysing and predicting behaviour of software architectures. *Journal of Integrated Design and Process Science, 5*(3), 25–51.

Stohl, C. (2001). Globalizing organizational communication. In E. M. Jablin & L. L. Putman (Eds.), *The new handbook of organizational communication: Advances in theory, research, and methods* (pp. 323–375). Thousand Oaks, CA: Sage.

Thomas, L. T., & Ganster, D. C. (1995). Impact of family-supportive work variables on work-family conflict and strain: A control perspective. *Journal of Applied Psychology, 80*(1), 6–15.

Thompson, J. D. (1967). *Organizations in action*. McGraw-Hill.

Thompson, C. A., Jahn, E. W., Kopelman, R. E., & Prottas, D. J. (2004). Perceived organizational family support: A longitudinal and multilevel analysis. *Journal of Managerial Issues, 16*(4), 545–565.

Tripp, J. F., Riemenschneider, C., & Thatcher, J. B. (2016). Job satisfaction in agile development teams: Agile development as work redesign. *Journal of Association for Information Systems, 17*(4), 267–307.

Walsham, G. (1997). Actor-network theory and I.S. research: Current status and future prospects. *Information systems and qualitative research* (466–480). Springer.

Xia, W., & Lee, G. (2005). Complexity of information systems development projects: Conceptualization and measurement development. *Journal of Management Information Systems, 22*(1), 45–83.

CHAPTER 3

The Border Crosser's Characteristics and Work–Life Conflict

In the previous chapter, we examined the effects of a number of factors that impact the WLC of IT professionals involved in globally distributed work. Drawing on Border Theory, the factors discussed were related to the border keepers' roles, the flexibility, and permeability of the borders, and the characteristics of the domain. In this chapter, we focus on the effect of *border crossers'* (i.e., the IT professionals') characteristics on their work–life conflict (WLC).[1]

Although this book is primarily focused on how companies and managers can create environments which can help in minimizing WLC, it is nevertheless helpful to discuss some *individual-level characteristics* which might contribute to that end. We do emphasize that many of the attributes of the border crosser discussed here are traits that are

[1] We note that for this book, as explained in Chapter 1, we see high work–life conflict (WLC) as low work–life balance (WLB). In other words, the two constructs are seen as being on the same continuum, on opposing sides.

Some of the material in this paper has been taken from the paper: Sarker, Saonee, Sarker, Suprateek, Ondrus, Jan, Jana, Debasish, and Ahuja, Manju. (2011). The Role of Individual, Family-Related, and Organizational Factors in Shaping WLC in Offshoring Contexts: A Study of European and Indian IT Professionals. PACIS Proceedings.

S. Sarker et al., *Navigating Work and Life Boundaries*,
https://doi.org/10.1007/978-3-030-72759-8_3

not easy to change in the short-run and deliberate attempts to change or "manipulate" them in certain contexts may be seen as unfair and discriminatory.

Individual-level variables that have been explored in the academic literature are associated with, for instance: (a) employees having personal commitments such as young children or other stressful situations at home (Ahuja et al., 2015); (b) gender impacts where the society may not encourage women employees working late (Sarker et al., 2018); (c) particular personality traits of employees that may lend themselves to stress (Poelmans et al., 2009), and (d) certain roles of employees that demand coordination across multiple time zones and locations (Sarker et al., 2010), all of which can potentially increase WLC.

As in the case of Chapter 2, this chapter draws much of its inspiration from our research conducted in the distributed IT work, specifically, globally distributed software development (GDSD). The unique nature of this type of work, which includes challenges such as long working hours, project complexity, separation by time and space, changing requirements, and potential for scope creep (Sarker et al., 2018), provides insights that can apply to many other types of work environments. In-depth interviews of managers and software developers (described in Appendix 1) who work under these conditions lent further credibility to the role of the above-mentioned factors.

Key Influencing Characteristics of the Border Crosser

As mentioned earlier, there are several individual-level differences that may increase the possibility of WLC such as caregiving responsibilities which require time and energy to manage (Ahuja et al., 2015), gender-related expectations, especially related to "appropriate" feminine behavior, and inherent ability to handle stress (Poelmans et al., 2009). In this chapter, we specifically address the effects of the following: gender, neuroticism, relationship status, caregiving role, priority of time with family, nature of the professional role (that is, technical or not), and culture. The importance of these factors was emphasized by our interviewees.

Gender

Traditionally, literature on WLB/WLC has tended to place an emphasis on the role gender and family status play in increasing conflict between work and life demands (e.g., Greenhaus & Beutell, 1985; Poelmans et al., 2009). Although couples have become more egalitarian in recent years, gender roles and expectations appear to persist. Allen et al. (2020) suggest that gender egalitarianism plays a role in work demands as well as micro-role transitions (Ashforth et al., 2000), which in turn affects WLC. At the same time, there is evidence in WLC research that suggests mixed results with regard to gender, and researchers (e.g., Allen et al., 2020; Rajadhyaksha et al., 2017) recommend that considering gender in conjunction with other contextual factors such as culture provide more accurate results. To this end, we have also included national culture as an additional variable here.

Three themes which stood out in our interviews include: differing expectations between men and women, the strains related to being a working mom, and mothers facing the decision of whether to continue an outside job or spend more time at home with their children.

First, expectations were different, or at least perceived to be different for men and women. A male software production planner in Denmark reflected on traditional expectations of women and how that might impact their WLC. Specifically, he referred to:

> ...children, housekeeping, shopping, those traditional roles that we've been seeing women in, and then on top of this, they're expected to be as active as their male colleagues.

This perception was formed after seeing male coworkers participating in their internal messaging platform at all hours of the night. On the other hand, a female program manager in Denmark suggested that women, more than men, were more likely to have their decision to not participate in an after-hours work activity respected. She shared that, as a woman, she could expect that her coworkers would respect her decision to spend time with her family; however, a man who made the same decision might not be respected as much. This is not to say that men do not play a role in raising children. A male senior application development administrator in the United States reflected on his experiences of working from home as a father:

> … I like the fact that I'm always home when my kids are home, whether I'm interacting with them or not. If they need something, I'm there.

Second, based in part on these differing expectations, the interviewees perceived that it was more difficult for mothers to manage these demands while also maintaining a full-time job. A male Sr. staff firmware engineer in the United States suggested that the traditional roles of women that require them to take care of family-related events often increase their WLC. He stated:

> … my impression is …that women in general have a lot more family-oriented things that they have to sacrifice during work hours. …

In India, a female HR business partner team lead expressed that so much depends on:

> …how supportive our spouses are, how supportive our family is… I find that being a mom, I'm more like 'I need to be home more' or 'Nine to five is what I can work… definitely, I think for working moms it needs more balancing.

Finally, due to family demands and a desire to spend more time with their children, some women choose to step away from the workforce for some years in their lives. Career goals may be different for women. When asked whether she thought women were "uniquely equipped to handle work life challenges," a female process documentation specialist from the United States reflected that, when the time came around, she wanted to eventually be able to stay home with her children. A male lab services specialist shared a similar perspective:

> … my own colleagues' wives in good positions in the IT industry, give up their jobs… …because you have to do the balancing… So, if you ask me, between men and women, where I think that the problem remains, especially in India, I think it's definitely more evident. However, the compromise happens, the woman makes the compromise…

Past research also suggests that gender can affect WLC in different ways, illustrated by the mixed results in the extant literature. While some researchers have suggested that gender does not have a significant effect on WLC, others have emphatically argued (consistent with our interviewees quoted earlier) that gender does play an important role, with female employees experiencing greater WLC than male employees (e.g., Lyness & Kropf, 2005). Greenhaus & Powell (2006, p. 72) argue that "individuals who participate in multiple roles (such as work and family) inevitably experience conflict and stress that detract from their quality of life." Past research shows that women often need to play both roles simultaneously, and hence they experience higher conflicts. Kossek et al., (1999, p. 110) state that "women consistently work more hours (combined paid and unpaid), spend more time on family responsibilities, and experience greater role overload and work-family conflict." In fact, prior studies note that in "dual earner families with multiple children, women worked ninety hours a week (combined paid and unpaid chores) compared with sixty hours for men" (Kossek et al., 1999, p. 110). In the context of IT work, Quesenberry et al. (2006) argue that women experience higher work–family conflicts since they find it extremely difficult to balance "domestic responsibilities while trying to keep pace with a rapidly changing field" (p. 136). Thus, we have:

H1: *Compared to male IT professionals, female IT professionals involved in globally distributed IT work will experience higher WLC.*

Neuroticism

In the nature versus nurture debate, research has investigated the effects of genetic foundations of several potentially stress-relevant personality traits, including harm avoidance, impulsiveness, risk perception, and positive emotionality. In a review of the genetic and environmental influences on human psychological difference, Bouchard and McGue (2003) conclude that "there is strong evidence that … psychological differences, when reliably measured, are moderately to substantially heritable" (p. 4). Our respondents indicated that certain personalities may be better suited for distributed IT work. For instance, one said:

> Stresses are there... Right?... it basically depends on the individuals and the individualistic personality also. That they tend to create ... conflicts. And at that time, we generally utilize program management...

However, other personalities may have a more difficult time managing such pressures. Neuroticism shows the strongest effects in this regard, and is used here as an example of a personality trait with major implications for stress perceptions and, consequently, WLC. Neuroticism refers to "anxiety, insecurity, defensiveness, tension and worry" (Wayne et al., 2004, p. 112). Neurotics spend more time focusing on "worrying," and developing "negative affect" (Wayne et al., 2004, p. 112), and less time on accomplishing their tasks both at home or at work. Not surprisingly, neurotics are known to face more family and work-related stress, which translates to increased WLC (Stoeva et al., 2002). Given that neuroticism is a personality-related characteristic, its effect on an individual's WLC is likely to manifest itself irrespective of the work context. Thus, we have:

H2: *Neuroticism in IT professionals involved in globally distributed IT work will be positively associated with WLC.*

Relationship Status

Software development companies involved in globally distributed work tend to have professional cultures where staying late, working through weekends, and taking calls during what is traditionally considered personal time are commonplace, and often expected. Workers who are single and who do not have conflicting demands at home are more likely to be able to deal with this. Cohabitation, in general, and being married, specifically, is likely to result in higher WLC for such workers because partner/spouse expectations tend to create competing demands on their time and attention, resulting in higher levels of WLC. Their client counterparts will see similar effects. In this regard, one of our respondents said:

> I guess being single and – well, I'm not young anymore – but reasonably young makes it easier to do odd hours or staying later just because you're not constrained by anybody else's schedule.

Another mentioned:

> I do have one colleague who is single and he's one of the people who goes into the office… I think, it's mostly just for social interaction. And as opposed to myself, raising children, where I do have social contact with my family regularly.

Yet another said:

> ...if you treat it on the gender basis, it does become a problem for the female counterparts, but bachelors [men], say young people coming out of college and [with] probably, at the most, one year of experience ...those people.. don't really have problems.

Individuals in relationships, and thinking of starting a family, face additional concerns. In an interview in Denmark, one female IT professional suggested that:

> ... in the later point in life where we probably have children, I think I would probably pursue maybe less challenges work-wise because I know that my kids will probably take up more time and I want to spend more time [with them]...

Based on the above, we have:

H3: *IT professionals involved in globally distributed IT work who are married (or have a significant other) will experience higher WLC, compared to those who are unmarried (or do not have a significant other).*

Caregiving Role

Previous literature has provided evidence related to caregiving roles contributing to WFC (Allen et. al., 2020). This relationship is likely to be even stronger among globally distributed IT workers because of the intensity of the work environment, the potential of 24 × 7 connectivity, the extent of change these workers must deal with, and the need for continuous learning. Riemenschneider and Armstrong (forthcoming) have showed these factors to be distinctive characteristics of the IT profession in general, that differentiate IT work from other types of work in organizations. This work environment is focused around a complex, multifaceted knowledge base, and continuous adaptation of that knowledge base. In addition, the globally distributed IT workers must deal with time zone differences. Such a domain becomes challenging for individuals who have parenting and other caregiving responsibilities. A software developer in the United States specifically suggested that the type of work he did was better for those who were single, rather than those with family or other caregiving commitments, which might constrain availability.

Some individuals might choose to step back from intense work. A mother in India shared that her job had allowed flexibility, which enabled her to return to work after the birth of her first child. However, she chose to take a sabbatical after her second child seemed to get upset and screamed each time when she tried to drop him off at daycare. In another interview, a supply center manager in Denmark shared a story about a content writer who, after two years of successful work, chose to step out of a role that required distributed work after he became a father. The new father told his manager that it would be impossible for him to work under the pressure he had been under, and also *be* a father.

A senior software tester from India suggested that having a family, especially in situations where both parents are working, may result in less flexibility to work beyond a traditional schedule. He noted that this is particularly problematic in the software development industry, where team members may be working in multiple time zones. In these cases, working beyond traditional hours may be the only way to meet synchronously with other team members who are working on the same project. His perception was that, in these situations, WLB would be adversely affected.

Although working from home is often presented as a way to help manage WLB, a male software engineer in the United States found that being a father changed the way he was able to work from home. Prior to having a child, he would often catch up at night on projects. But after he had a son, he is not able to do so:

> ...now it's hard because at 5 o'clock I have to be done for the day because I have run upstairs and watch him as my wife goes to work in the evening. So that sort of break, where I'm forced to take that break, sometimes I won't be able to let stuff go and as soon as he goes to bed, I run right back downstairs to start on the stuff again.

This resulted in feelings of guilt both about working from home (while others in his company are not allowed to) and for feeling distracted by work situations during family time, resulting in perceptions of high WLC.

A female program manager shared a story about a woman she knew who had two small children, in addition to holding a job which came with big responsibilities, including evening meetings, travel, and, on top of that, a commute of almost an hour. The manager suggested that this coworker was likely experiencing significant conflict between her work and family roles.

As the above examples highlight, caregiving roles can have severe implications for the WLC of employees (Lyness & Kropf, 2005, p. 43). Researchers such as Greenhaus and Beutell (1985) and Netemeyer et al. (2004) argue that individuals who have families tend to have their family demands interfere with their job performance, and this enhances their WLC. Caregiving tasks range from not only "Activities of Daily Living (ADLs) such as eating, dressing, bathing," etc., but also Instrumental Activities of Daily Living (IADLs) such as companionship, and transportation (Kossek et al., 1999, p. 116). Increases in job demands or ADLs and IADLs can cause serious WLC. Such a conflict appears to be common in the offshoring context, wherein individuals are often required to work at times that are traditionally allocated for personal activities and set aside for families. Thus, we have:

H4: *IT professionals involved in globally distributed IT work who have caregiving responsibilities will experience higher WLC, compared to those who do not.*

Priority of Time with Family

Recent research argues that it is not only the existence of family and caregiving responsibilities, but the important one puts on time with family that affects the WLC (e.g., Aryee et al., 2005). Individuals involved in distributed IT work—due to time and space distances with their remote counterparts—often need to work during hours which may be considered "leisure time" in the traditional work perspective. If that leisure time is considered important for that individual, he/she is likely to experience more conflict.

Our respondents indicated that sometimes the priority of time is dictated by family roles and societal expectations. A program manager in Denmark expressed her perception that men seem to have an easier time prioritizing work over family, while women are expected to prioritize family time, going as far as to say that:

> … I have met a lot of men in my career that is completely dedicated and don't recognize they actually have a family.

If an employee values his/her time with family highly, he/she will view any other role-defined activity, especially when it spills over its normal boundaries, as *interference*, and preventing him/her from enjoying the leisure (Aryee et al., 2005). If this time is "sacred" for them, then any work-related task overflowing into this time will be seen as a source of work–life conflict. Thus, we argue:

H5: *IT professionals involved in globally distributed IT work who put higher priority on their time with family will experience higher WLC, compared to those who put lower priority on their time with family.*

Technical Versus Managerial Role

We expect that managers would be among those who experience greater conflicts between work and life spheres because they have higher levels of responsibility across different tasks and functions. A male lab services and solutions group team member in India expressed the view that managers experience greater demands with respect to balancing life and work domains. He specifically argued that various issues contribute to these demands, namely workload management, people management, and interfacing with top management regarding the status of projects. A female desk manager in India shared that instead of taking weekends off, she used the time for "catching up on the people management responsibilities, which took a back seat because our focus is release management." Project managers also share this burden. A male supply chain manager in Denmark emphasized the impact of distributed work on the WLC of project managers:

> The more distributed it gets, the more horrendous it is to manage the project plan because if you really care for your project, then you have to be available and you have to be talking to all these different people who own different pieces in different parts of the world.

Technical workers, in general, appear to be better able to manage their WLC. A male HR team member in India mentioned that when jobs were technically focused rather than relationship-focused and were planned neatly in shifts (rather than overflowing across shifts, as is typical of relationship-focused responsibilities), employees are able to work:

> ...eight hours and after the eight hours the next person will come and relieve him.
> So, it's well planned ... You can plan your leave. You can plan your holidays.

Thus, we have:

H6: *IT professionals involved in globally distributed IT work holding managerial roles will experience higher WLC than those holding technical roles.*

National Context

It is a well-known fact that India is considered to be one of the most attractive IT offshoring destinations, and that many India-based professionals are engaged in (or working in) distributed projects with collaborators across the globe. A recent report by Gartner indicates a strong increase of several European nations as attractive offshoring locations. Further, many European IT workers serve as a "bridge" (Olsson Holmström et al., 2008), and others may participate in distributed IT projects with counterparts from, for example, Asia and/or the Americas. What these studies highlight is that we are likely to find a number of IT professionals not only in India but also in Europe who are involved with IT professionals from North America in projects across distributed locations.

A meta-analysis by Allen et al. (2020) has shown that while domain demands strongly predict WLC across countries, national culture also influences this relationship. For instance, they found the relationship between WLC and satisfaction outcomes was significant across regions, except South Asia, a region that has been described as highly group-oriented, humane, male-dominated, and hierarchical. The findings of the meta-analysis suggest that relationships between WLC and satisfaction outcomes are weaker in societies that are more collectivistic and exhibit higher power distance than those that are more individualistic and exhibit lower power distance.

Thus, given the above and other differences in culture, labor practices, spaces and infrastructures at home, and institutional environments such as labor laws between the United States, Europe, and Asia, significant differences in WLC can be expected (Sarker et al., 2018).

In our interviews, a Danish manager, for example, reflected on the different attitudes toward work–life balance in different countries as well as companies.

> ... work-life balance and comes down to, of course, the country, culture, country, setting, like you also mentioned, since we live in Denmark, so how does it go there.

In addition, different countries and cultures have different expectations regarding working hours. A male software production planner in Denmark specifically suggested that he had noticed differences in the hours Scandinavians worked versus other cultures. This was reiterated by a male supply chain manager in Denmark who noted:

> A huge difference between how Americans perceive work life... From what I understand, it's much more likely for an American person working in a software company to work almost all the time, but in the case of Denmark, that is very less likely to happen; most people focus much more on families and taking time out of work.

He also mentioned that in Denmark, there is a strong belief that an employee cannot be productive in the long run if they are working more than seven to eight hours a day:

> So even if you work, you are basically hurting yourself, either in the long run or in the short run, hurting your family, friends, and other interests and so on... So, calls in the evening or calls in the weekends or calls in the holidays, vacation period, that is not considered normal.

The supply chain manager from Denmark also mentioned that he perceived workers in India as having high WLC:

> ...for most people [in India] I have interacted with, work is much more prioritized than life is. The way we understand by term life and this work-life context with having time out with family, friends or going out on vacations, stuff like that is always low prioritized.

This appears to be changing, however. An internal organizational analyst in India reflected on the fact that concerns about work–life balance is diffusing into the Indian workplaces.

Furthermore, WLC can be affected because of different levels of expectations in different countries. A male design manager in India shared his views about some of these differences:

> ...when you work with U.S., everything is very formal and you have to follow things very strictly. It's not like they are strict with a schedule, but then it has to be systematic. There has to be documentation. There has to be design and then it to be good enough. And when it comes to our European partners, the expectation is something different, especially with Barcelona. We have very get going, get going, don't stop. ...Okay, documentation we'll do it, we'll do it, but first let's have the code ready, let's have it ready and we'll work it out later. ... without documentation you can still live, but in a place like India, that's a big no no

Different countries do have different norms of work and expectations and these can, directly or indirectly, lead to different levels of WLC. Also, in line with the metaphor of border crossing, Ashforth et al. (2000) offered a conjecture that the culture in which individuals are embedded may affect border management processes because culture reflects norms and expectations that guide how individuals separate, define, and draw borders (or boundaries) between interpersonal relationships and different roles. Thus, we have:

H7: *The national context in which the IT professionals involved in globally distributed work are embedded in will affect the level of WLC.*

We sought to test the above hypotheses using data from a large-scale survey of IT professionals involved in distributed work. The details of the survey are described in Appendix 3.

Measurement of Variables

We used established instruments (where possible) for measuring our constructs. WLC was measured using eight items adapted from Kopelman et al. (1983). Among the individual-level variables, neuroticism was measured using the Big Five Personality Scale's eight neuroticism items. Gender, family structure, functional role, and national context were assessed using single item measures. Priority of time with family was measured using three items that captured (on a scale of 1 to 7, where 1 referred to "Not at all" and 7 referred to "To a great extent") the extent to which individuals valued their time and involvement in family life, and their interests centered around family. The multi-item scales demonstrated good validity with Cronbach's alpha of 0.925 (WLC), 0.861 (priority of time with family), and 7380 (Neuroticism), respectively.

Results

PLS-Graph Version 3.00 (Build 1126) was used for analyzing the data. Our results are summarized in Table 3.1. Among the individual-level variables, neuroticism had significant effects on WLC. With respect to

Table 3.1 Results of PLS-graph analysis—The influence of border crosser's characteristics on work–life conflict (R^2: 0.245)

Hypothesis #	*Independent variable and operationalization*	*Descriptive*	*Nature of result (β; significance level)*
H1	Gender 1. Male 2. Female	Male—767 Female—233	0.034; ns
H2	Neuroticism		0.449; $p < 0.01$; Supported
H3	Relationship status) 1. Not married 2. Married	Not married—384 Married—616	0.019; ns
H4	Taking Care of dependents 1. Yes 2. No	Yes—498 No—502	−0.076; $p < 0.05$; Supported
H5	Priority of time with family		0.084; $p < 0.01$; Supported
H6	Role 0 Non-technical 1 Technical	Non-technical—250 Technical—750	−0.034; ns
H7	National context 1 India 2 UK 3 USA	India—249 UK—2s51 USA—500	−099; $p < 0.01$; Supported

the family-related variables, both family structure (that is, the existence of a family), and priority of time with family had a positive association with WLC, as expected. Gender, relationship status, and role showed no effect on WLC. We also examined the effects of national context in which the workers were embedded, and found that national context (where the individual is embedded) does determine the level of WLC experienced.

Discussion

In H1, we proposed that female IT professionals involved in globally distributed IT work would experience higher WLC. Our results, however, found that gender had no effect on WLC. This is not entirely inconsistent with prior research, which often argues that "women have been socialized over the generations to the nurturing role of the family. No matter how achievement orientated the women is," she is able to balance these two domains more easily (Gambles et al., 2006, p. 77). Korabik et al. (2003) also report from their focus group studies that women tend to be better at multitasking than men, as a result they are able to "fulfill many work and family duties without much support (p. 294)," and not be burdened by (and hence perceive) the conflict between the two domains. Our findings can also be explained by a self-selection effect such that women who survive this IT profession (especially involving globally distributed work) are able to handle two different domains of responsibilities as well as men.

As per H2, our results suggest that individuals who were high on neuroticism perceived to have more WLC than those who scored low on this trait. Neurotics tend to focus too much on issues that might not be related to actual work. They lose energy and time trying to understand or solve these issues instead of completing their assigned tasks in a punctual manner. Furthermore, neurotic people have more difficulties in separating problems they have at work and at home. This also contributes to higher levels of stress and a negative state of mind that create WLC.

No relationship was found between the IT professionals' relationship status (i.e., married or not) and WLC. This was inconsistent with H3. It appears that partner demands do not have an effect on WLC. Our results indicate that the household help and social support that may be available to married workers from their spouses may contribute to their WLB. It is also possible that many of our respondents have working partners and they are both burning the midnight oil. This could mean that they are able to effectively negotiate their balancing of work and life.

Caregiving status, on the other hand, did significantly affect WLC (H4). As past research has indicated, employees with families tend to face more demands in their caregiving roles (Kossek et al., 1999). The demands of the family domain coupled with the intense demands at the workplace that general IT workers specifically engaged in distributed work face cause serious WLC (Messersmith, 2007). Further, as per H5, we found that IT workers in our study who valued their leisure time and privileged the family and time spent with family experienced higher WLC.

We had expected that IT workers involved in managerial roles will experience higher WLC (H6). Our survey results do not support this. While managers have higher levels of responsibilities, they may also be better compensated as a result of which they may be better able to hire help. Similarly, they may have better working conditions even when they are working from home. Further, they have higher job autonomy. These factors might balance each other, resulting in a nonsignificant effect.

Some of the interview subjects had plenty to say about this. For example, a male product manager in India suggested that managers are often forced to be better planners and thus may not experience higher WLC:

> Management people don't have a choice. Right? We just have to plan for it. This is due to an infrequent need to attend meetings. I mean they may get into a meeting once in a while to hash things out and then that's it, they're set for the next couple of months...they don't have to worry about it.

However, others noted that assumption that technical roles offer lower WLC may not necessarily be true. For example, workers engaged in technical roles and using agile methodologies needed to be available for scrum meetings during personal time, and experienced higher WLC. A female HR team leader in India shared about the occasional necessity for the development team to work after hours due to testing needs. While it stands to reason that there are some roles which appear to have a higher probability of experiencing conflicts between work and home spheres, perhaps it is a matter of individual choice, related to (as some have suggested) whether or not the individual is seeking rapid advancement in the company.

A male community learning manager in India suggested that to have a job which requires 24X7 availability is a matter of choice. He shared the opinion that "it [WLC] happens only when you really want to grow faster than others after achieving something…" Along similar lines, while noting his company's respect for diversity and WLB, a male supply chain manager in Denmark noted:

> I think it's expected that if you want to grow fast, then you need to be available. So, the way to put that would be that if you're not always available when you're required, then it can hurt your career because things won't stop. If there are deadlines to be met, there are deadlines to be met…

However, others, such as this female desk manager in India, disagreed with this view, and suggested:

> career progression happens more from … what value you're able to give in your current job. And first of all, I think career progression is all about being in the right place at the right time. Are you in the right place where there is growth going to happen and anticipate it and doing the right things? So, I don't think just by working 60 months [hours a week] or taking up some very high visibility role and a high pressure role, one will move [up]. I don't think so. There is also a factor of being in the right place and also position yourself appropriately and see that there is growth happening.

A male installation and licensing team member in India, who was formally in a role as an individual contributor (rather than manager others or working as part of team), suggested that there were periods when he experienced high WLC and periods when that was not the case. WLC may have more to do with nature of the project demands and other factors discussed in Chapter 2, rather than the role.

> I think the work-life balance is not bad at all. In the beginning there were times when we used to work on weekends. But now for the past couple of years, we are not doing weekends or not spending more than eight hours.

All too often, exercising the choice of whether or not to be available at odd hours can be viewed as an indicator of the worker's desire to seek advancement in the company. Based on signaling and attributions theories, this is referred to as "work devotion attribution" (Bourdeau et al., 2019). Positive judgment in this regard made by the supervisor leads to good career outcomes, a negative attribution can lead to negative outcomes for the individual.

Finally, we found that WLC is related to the national context, with respondents from India reporting the highest WLC, those from United Kingdom in the middle, and the respondents from United States reporting the lowest on an average within the three countries. A number of factors might contribute to this finding. Many of the companies from which respondents were drawn were US-based, so it is likely that scheduling was dictated by US-based times, and thus the US professionals had more control of their schedule and may have organized meetings and synchronous sessions based on their convenience. Second, in the case of India, interviewees suggested that working from home was not common, and the absence of demarcated workspace in the home increased the necessity of being present in an office in order to participate in conference calls or take care of issues with the code collaboratively with distributed overseas colleagues (Sarker et al., 2018).

Third, IT workers in India typically have long working hours (Gambles et al., 2006), and are considered to be devoted workers (Hofstede, 2001). This finding is consistent with the long-term orientation dimension of Hofstede (2001), on which India scores highly. In such cultures, organizations and governments tend to value leisure time much less than other cultures and does not make a concerted effort to protect the leisure time for the employees. Thus, if an IT worker values his/her leisure time individually, or has several social obligations to meet (e.g., Hofstede, 2001), they are left to fend for themselves, and are hence likely to experience more WLC.

The work pattern in Europe is quite different. According to Hofstede's (2001) study, most European nations score much lower on the long-term orientation dimension. Such national cultures value leisure time in general. Consequently, the work schedules and expectations are far less demanding than in India. Moreover, in the case of distributed IT work which often involves offshoring between United States, United Kingdom, and India, professionals in United Kingdom had large overlaps of working hours with both the US and Indian counterparts, and are thus less vulnerable to needing to work at odd hours compared to the Indian colleagues.

Additional Results: The Effect of WLC on Performance and Turnover

One might recall that in Chapter 1, we discussed that WLB/WLC can impact several outcomes such as performance and turnover intentions. In this chapter, we also examine if that is indeed the case, and if gender and national context play a role.

We found that high WLC was associated with intention to leave the company in general, irrespective of the national context or gender. This result should be seen as a clear message that for companies interested in maintaining a stable workforce involved in globally distributed work, it is absolutely essential to manage the level of WLC.

With respect to the effect of high WLC on performance, the results were interesting. WLC had no effect on the performance for respondents from the United States and United Kingdom; however, performance for respondents from India increased with higher WLC (marginal effect). In addition, with respect to the effect of WLC on performance by gender, there was no effect for males; however, the performance of females went up, at least in the short run (our data being cross-sectional, we are not able to say much about the long-term effects).

While it would be easy to interpret these findings to mean that women's performance increases with high WLC, we would caution against such a conclusion. Indeed, it is a common belief that women with nonwork responsibilities/conflict also learn how to manage work more efficiently in order to get things done, and that may also help in performance. However, given that this is a cross-sectional rather than a longitudinal study, these results likely indicate that compared to men, high-performing women experience higher levels of WLC. This conjecture is consistent with other research showing that those who substantially exceed work-related responsibilities and performance are more likely to experience work–family conflict, and that this is particularly true for women (Bolino & Turnley, 2005). Alternatively, those with higher level of conflict at home might take solace in work and overwork to avoid conflict home although this is likely to be the case for both genders. It is important to remember that IT industry is largely male-dominated and women might feel the pressure to overwork to fit in and be "one of the boys," which may result in sacrificing home life to some extent. Bolino and Turnley (2005) also found that the personal cost of citizenship behavior is higher for women. Similarly, Offer and Schneider (2011) found that mothers were more likely than fathers to multitask at home as well as in public, creating more WLC and consequently, adversely affecting their own well-being. India being a more male-dominated society, women in India likely perform a high higher portion of the housework than women in United States or United Kingdom. This could explain why this relationship is even more pronounced for them.

Given the above, we would caution organizations to conclude that high WLC for women would lead to higher performance by them. In the interest of encouraging more women to enter and persist in the IT profession in general, and offshoring in specific, it would behoove firms to create conditions for long-term success of women in the industry, including conditions for a balanced work and life (Ahuja, 2002; Armstrong & Giddens, 2018). We discuss this further in guideline 2.

Implications

This chapter has presented individual-level factors that can be associated with higher levels of WLC (Jessup & Robey, 2002). We further suggest that some of these factors create a chain that can ultimately affect job-related outcomes.

Many of our findings confirm previously found relationships across cultural contexts, while others were found to be moderated by culture (Gibson et al., 2009). This is important because previous research has revealed limitations of treating work–family research as universally applicable. Second, our bottom-up approach using interviews, helps aggregate lower level properties of the phenomena and also highlights the influence of higher level contextual factors on lower levels of the system (Kozlowski & Klein, 2000). This complements extant research within the work–family domain that has typically approached studies in terms of understanding how societal values or organizational policies influence individual phenomena such as WLC.

Based on the empirical results and discussion in this chapter, we advocate a broadening of the vision of workplace goals. These should include the notions of WLC that take into account the "whole person." By doing so, we expand the nomological network of what a productive workforce can achieve by leveraging core elements of well-being for achieving performance and productivity while enjoying a more satisfying, fulfilling, and healthier life. All of these outcomes contribute to more effective human resource strategies and, ultimately, to organizational competitiveness.

Guideline 1: Provide a Menu of Job Designs to Account for Current Realities of Life

One implication for organizations is to recognize that while some of the factors we presented are traits or simple facts of life (e.g., gender, caregiving role, relationship status), others entail making choices (e.g., priority of time with family, functional role) by the individual or the organization. In addition to making choices, employees must reckon with their shifting identities to account for their changing life circumstances over time. In order to accommodate factors that are "given," it would befit organizations to provide a menu of job designs to account for current realities of life that the employees might be facing. Similarly, evolving phases of life can be accommodated by such a menu of job designs and work arrangements.

Guideline 2: Play the Long Game by "investing" in WLC Policies

Organizations need to recognize that WLC and stress have an incremental, cumulative, and long-term effect. Our respondents indicated that most people are not aware of the incremental effects of these micro-stress events because they believe that they are managing their workload. While this is true, the constant state of hyperactivity takes its toll over time and can have long-term negative effects of lower commitment, higher turnover, employee disconnectedness, disengagement, and burnout.

A study of Indian IT developers involved in offshoring (Sarker et al., 2010) showed that in the long term, WLC can even influence the valence of these professionals toward the type of job (e.g., globally distributed IT work), not just the organization. This type of high turnover can cost organizations in recruiting, training, and onboarding. Deleterious effects on valence might result in, for example, women or even male professionals with caregiving responsibilities to exit the profession, creating a shortage of software development talent, which can result in higher turnover of IT professionals across the industry and the skyrocketing of salaries that would make industries less competitive.

By paying attention to short-term well-being of the worker, long-term negative effects can be mitigated and the balance can be tilted in favor of the positive implications. Our advice to organizations, therefore, is to be proactive in addressing work–life issues, and considering WLB initiatives to be an investment in their workforce rather than as a cost.

Guideline 3: Guard Against the "Work-Devotion" Attributions

Another guideline we offer is to guard against the attributions of employees' "work devotion" if they seek a balanced work–life. Many times, companies offer policies to aid WLB but when employees take advantage of these, their work devotion can be questioned. Bourdeau et. al. (2019) have shown that the supervisors' attributions related to work devotion can result in either positive and negative career consequences for users of work–life policies, depending on work devotion norms prevalent in the organization. This should be considered in policy designs as well as implementation. Organizations should also guard against relying on false proxies for reputation, such as gender, race, and caregiving situations.

Guideline 4: Provide Cultural Sensitivity and Communication Training to Offshoring Workers

We have also discussed the effects of the national and cultural context in which an individual (and their distributed collaborator) is embedded in. In entering offshoring arrangements, organizations should not only take into account the employment laws but also cultural differences among the countries. These differences are important to understand as this can help offshoring companies with understanding cross-cultural effects with regard to work–life conflict and find ways of addressing these differences (Ollier-Malaterre, 2016). For instance, there may be differences among cultures with respect to timeliness, the tendency to say "yes" even when the deadlines proposed are unachievable. One harmful effect of cultural differences is the ingroup–outgroup effect where team members tend to attribute any mishaps that occur to the outgroup, thereby leading to strain-based as well as behavior-based stress, and consequently WLC (Greenhaus & Beutell, 1985). By providing sensitivity training and communication, training, some of these effects can be mitigated.

Chapter Conclusion

In this chapter, we have provided an overview of various aspects of the individual IT professional (or border crosser) that may adversely affect their WLC. The specific variables presented were gender, personality factors, relationship status, caregiving roles, functional roles, and finally culture. In terms of culture, a meta-analysis by Allen et al. (2020) suggests that with some exceptions, South Asia as a region has not received much attention in the WLC research. By focusing on this region, our research contributes to the WLC stream by addressing this gap.

Finally, the broader point this chapter seeks to highlight is that in terms of WLC management, it is important for organizations to attend to the "whole person," which includes the individual and key elements of his/her context.

References

Ahuja, M. (2002). Women in the information technology profession: A literature review, synthesis and research agenda. *European Journal of Information Systems, 11*(1), 20–34.

Ahuja, M. K., Goyal, S., Saunders, C., & Rutkowsi, A.F. (2015). The effect of technology on well-being: The 'dark' side and the 'bright' side.

Allen, T. D., French, K. A., Dumani, S., & Shockley, K. M. (2020). A cross-national meta-analytic examination of predictors and outcomes associated with work-family conflict. *Journal of Applied Psychology*. Advance online publication. https://doi.org/10.1037/apl0000442.

Armstrong D., & Giddens, L. (2018). The advancement and persistence of women in the information technology profession: An extension of Ahuja's gendered theory of IT career stages, *Information Systems Journal*, *28*(6), 10821124.

Aryee, S., Srinivas, E. S., & Tan, H. H. (2005). Rhythms of life: Antecedents and outcomes of work-family balance in employed parents. *Journal of Applied Psychology, 90*(1), 132–146.

Ashforth, B. E., Kreiner, G. E., & Fugate, M. (2000). All in a day's work: Boundaries and micro role transitions. *Academy of Management Review, 25*, 472–491.

Bolino, M. C., & Turnley, W. H. (2005). The personal costs of citizenship behavior: The relationship between individual initiative and role overload, job stress, and work-family conflict. *Journal of Applied Psychology, 90*(4), 740–748.

Bouchard Jr, T. J., & McGue, M. (2003). Genetic and environmental influences on human psychological differences. *Journal of Neurobiology, 54*(1), 4–45.

Bourdeau, S., Ollier-Malaterre, A., & Houlfort, N. (2019). Not all work-life policies are created equal: Career consequences of using enabling versus enclosing work-life policies. *Academy of Management Review, 44*(1), 172–193.

Gambles, R., Lewis, S., & Rapoport, R. (2006). *The myth of work-life balance: The challenge of our time for men, women, and societies*. John Wiley and Sons.

Gibson, C. B., Maznevski, M. L., & Kirkman, B. L. (2009). When does culture matter. In A. Y. Lewin (Ed.), *Emerging issues in international business* (pp. 46–70). Macmillan Press.

Greenhaus, J. H., & Beutell, N. J. (1985). Sources of conflict between work and family roles. *Academy of Management Review, 10*(1), 76–88.

Hofstede, G. (2001). *Culture's consequences: Comparing values, behaviors, institutions, and organizations across nations* (2nd ed.). Sage.

Jessup, L. M., & Robey, D. (2002). The relevance of social issues in ubiquitous computing environments. *Communications of the ACM, 45*(12), 88–91.

Kopelman, R. E., Greenhaus, J. H., & Connelly, T. E. (1983). A model of work, family, and interrole conflict: A construct validation study. *Organizational Behavior and Human Performance, 32*, 198–215.

Korabik, K., Lero, D. S., & Ayman, R. (2003). A multi-level approach to cross cultural work-family research: A micro and macro perspective. *International Journal of Cross Cultural Management, 3*(3), 289–303.

Kossek, E. E., Noe, R. A., & DeMarr, B. J. (1999). Work-family role synthesis: Individual and organizational determinants. *The International Journal of Conflict Management, 10*(2), 102–129.

Kozlowski, S. W. J., & Klein, K. J. (2000). A multilevel approach to theory and research in organizations: Contextual, temporal, and emergent processes. In K. J. Klein & S. W. J. Kozlowski (Eds.), *Multilevel theory, research and methods in organizations: Foundations, extensions, and new directions* (pp. 3–90). Jossey-Bass.

Lyness, K. S., & Kropf, M. B. (2005). Work-family balance: A study of European managers. *Human Relations, 58*(1), 33–60.

Messersmith, J. (2007). Managing WLC among information technology workers. *Human Resource Management, 46*(3), 429–451.

Netemeyer, R. G., Brashear-Alejandro, T., & Boles, J. S. (2004). A cross-national model of job-related outcomes of work role and family role variables: A retail sales context. *Journal of the Academy of Marketing Science, 32*(1), 49–60.

Offer, S., & Schneider, B. (2011). Revisiting the gender gap in time-use patterns: Multitasking and well-being among mothers and fathers in dual-earner families, *American Sociological Review, 76*(6), 809–833.

Ollier-Malaterre, A. (2016). Cross-national work-life research: A review at the individual level. In T. D. Allen & L. T. Eby (Eds.), *The Oxford handbook of work and family* (pp. 315–332). Oxford University Press.

Olsson Holmström, H., O Conchúir, E., Ågerfalk, P., & Fitzgerald, B. (2008). Two-stage offshoring: An investigation of the Irish bridge. *MIS Quarterly, 32*(2), 1–23.

Poelmans, S., Odle-Dusseau, H., & Beham, B. (2009). Work-life balance: Individual, organizational strategies and practices. In S. Cartwright & C. L. Cooper (Eds.), *The Oxford handbook of organizational well-being* (pp. 180–213). Oxford University Press.

Quesenberry, J. L., Trauth, E. M., & Morgan, A. J. (2006). Understanding the 'Mommy tracks': A framework for analyzing work-family balance in the IT workforce. *Information Resources Management Journal, 19*(2), 37–53.

Rajadhyaksha, U. (2017). Examining the interaction of societal culture and contextual variables on work-family conflict and work-family positive spillover. In K. Korabik, Z. Aycan & R. Ayman (Eds.), *The work-family interface in global context*. Routledge.

Riemenschneider, C., & D. Armstrong. (forthcoming). The development of the perceived distinctiveness antecedent of information systems professional identity. *MIS Quarterly*.

Sarker, S., Ahuja, M. K., & Sarker, S. (2018). Work-life conflict of distributed software development personnel: An empirical investigation using border theory. *Information Systems Research, 29*(1), 103126.

Sarker, S., Sarker, S., & Jana, D. (2010). The impact of the nature of globally distributed work arrangement on WLC and valence. *European Journal of Information Systems, 19*(2), 209–222.

Stoeva, A. Z., Chiu, R. K., & Greenhaus, J. H. (2002). Negative affectivity, role stress and work-family conflict. *Journal of Vocational Behavior,* 60(1), 116.

Wayne, J. H., Musisca, N., & Fleeson, W. (2004). Considering the role of personality in the work-family experience: Relationships of the big five to work-family conflict and facilitation. *Journal of Vocational Behavior, 64*(1), 108130.

CHAPTER 4

Global Offshoring of Systems Development and Work–Life Conflict: A Revelatory Case Study

Introduction

In the previous chapters, we focused on *factors* that appear to influence the work–life conflict (WLC) of *individuals*, and on specific individual-level outcomes. Moreover, we relied primarily on survey data, and interviews from different organizational contexts. In this chapter, we offer an in-depth, potentially revelatory case study, that takes a broader view on WLC, and highlights nuances such as the *changing nature* and *consequences of WLC*, that affect not only individual WLC experiences but also the relationship between offshore and onshore units—in terms of dependence, responsibility, and control. We believe that the above nuances are not easily captured through surveys based on past WLC literature or even with one-off interviews.

For many years, software development organizations have been engaging in offshoring practices. While the topic of offshoring is well

---

The chapter presents a revised version of an unpublished manuscript: Sarker, Suprateek, Sarker, Saonee, Jessup, Len, and Chakraborty, Suranjan. "Interpreting a case of IT offshore in-sourcing: A work–life balance perspective." An earlier version of the paper was presented at the *Academy of Management Annual Conference*, 2010.

S. Sarker et al., *Navigating Work and Life Boundaries*,
https://doi.org/10.1007/978-3-030-72759-8_4

understood by researchers and practitioners, one area that has not received much attention is the work–life conflict (WLC) or the work–life balance (WLB)[1] of the IT professionals involved in such arrangements. WLC has been seen to have serious negative effects, especially on the lives of IT workers who are involved in globally distributed IT projects with colleagues and clients separated by significant time and geographical/cultural distances. Through our case study, constructed using longitudinal data gathered from one of the divisions of a leading global company (pseudonym GLOBCOM), we attempt to offer a broad understanding of WLC issues related to IT offshoring, specifically in developing software in distributed settings around the globe.

Offshoring of IT work has been undertaken in two primary modes: outsourcing or insourcing. *Offshore outsourcing* refers to the shifting of work to third-party vendors overseas (Carmel & Agarwal, 2002). In such contexts, the third-party vendor is often responsible for a variety of IT-related functions for the outsourcing organization, and "hires, trains, supervises, and manages its [own] personnel" (Davis et al., 2006, p. 771). Such arrangements are seen as attractive, since they are perceived to be cost-effective, and enable the organization to profit from the rich IT skill-sets possessed by a large educated employee-pool in countries such as Russia, India, and China, where many of the offshore vendors are based. However, increased reliance on offshore outsourcing has made both practitioners and researchers wary of some serious pitfalls. Among the various documented downsides of offshore outsourcing are risks such as the potential loss of intellectual property and data of strategic importance, spillover of the domain knowledge to competitors (given that third-party vendors may work for several global organizations) and potential competitors, offshoring partners becoming competitors, problems associated with the lack of a common organizational culture, and so on (Patterson, 2006; Robinson & Kalakota, 2004).

To mitigate the risks mentioned above, some organizations started opting to "set-up service operations in the other countries" (Davis et al.,

[1] We remind the reader that while scholars are divided about this position, for this book, we adopt the view that WLB and WLC are related concepts on two opposite ends of a continuum. Please see Chapter 1 for a discussion of this issue. Essentially, WLC is said to occur when there is significant lack of balance in an individual's work and personal life domains, and vice versa. That is, high WLB is equivalent to low WLC, and the reverse is also true.

2006, p. 771). These offshore sites were treated as an "internal group within a global organization" (Carmel & Agarwal, 2002, p. 65), and the parent organization was to be responsible for every aspect of this center(s)' operations, including the hiring, supervision, management, and training of its personnel. The practice, termed as "offshore insourcing," enabled organizations to "reap the dual advantages of low-cost offshore environments and an internally controlled development environment" (Rao, 2004, p. 20). Given the increasing use of the insourcing strategy by several global IT organizations and the relative paucity of offshoring studies in the context of insourcing, we focus on this model.

Much of the existing literature on offshoring (be it insourcing or outsourcing) has focused on the benefits/disadvantages of this practice to the organizations, thereby closely examining the *financial* benefits, costs, and *risks* associated with this venture, the factors driving an organization's decision to outsource offshore, and developing strategies for effective management of offshore projects (e.g., Aron et al., 2005; Dutta & Roy, 2005; Levy, 2005; Patterson, 2006; Sakthivel, 2007). While acknowledging past contributions on instrumental aspects of offshoring, Niederman et al., (2006, p. 57), among others, urge future researchers to closely focus on the *working conditions* of the IT professionals who "are affected by offshoring in terms of their immediate and long-term employment."

One such *working condition*-related issue that is emerging as important in many organizations is the concept of *work–life conflict (WLC)* of its members. In today's competitive world, WLC has been seen to have significant effects on workers' health, general psychological well-being, and productivity (Felstead et al., 2002). This is also true for the IT workforce (Quesenberry et al., 2006), since workers need to adjust to the rapid pace and changing rhythms of IT work. The concept of WLC can be even more critical for IT workers who are involved in offshore projects with colleagues and clients separated by significant time and geographical/cultural distances; yet there are few academic explorations (if any) of this issue. In Fig. 4.1, we introduce work–life balance as a key element of the tension shaping issues related to offshoring. This is significant in the framing of the globally distributed software development (GDSD) or the IT (or other knowledge work) offshoring phenomenon since, until this point, researchers have generally approached the phenomenon from the economic and business risk/legal perspectives.

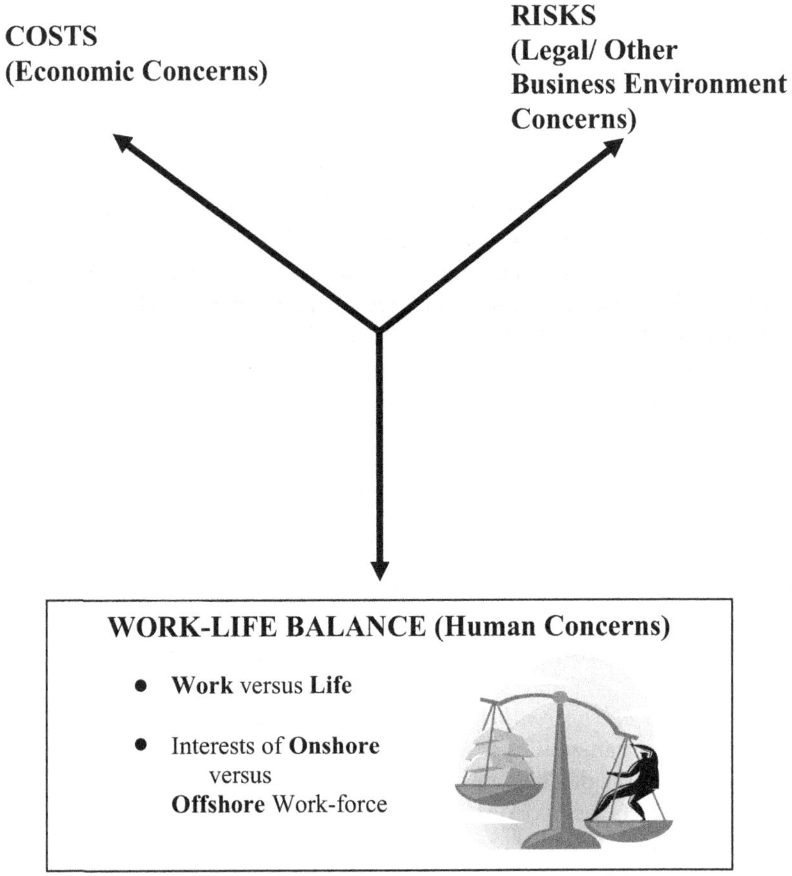

Fig. 4.1 The three key tensions in IT offshoring

Given the lack of theoretical frameworks on WLC issues in IT offshoring in general and offshore insourcing in particular, we develop our understanding inductively using data gathered from one of the divisions of a leading global IT company.

Orientation to the Case

The study derives its empirical material from the experiences of the B2B Systems division (a pseudonym for the focal division) of GLOBCOM (another pseudonym), a leading global company headquartered in the United States. The division studied is responsible for designing/developing systems that the company uses to manage its relationships with some of its significant business partners. The division initiated its offshoring efforts around 2002, and was making a conscious effort to manage not only its costs and productivity, but also to minimize the WLC of its employees, whom the organization's management rightly viewed as the most critical resource. Below, we interpretively reconstruct (Walsham 1995), based on our observations of GLOBCOM, the "stages" that organizations involved in offshore insourcing move through, with each stage presenting its own challenges to work–life balance. We note that, through this historical case, a number of issues emerge that remain relevant to an increasing number of businesses that are working in a distributed global context today. Methodological details related to this case are available in Appendix 1.

WLC and the (Re-)Structuring of the Insourcing Relationship: An Evolutionary Perspective

Next, we discuss how the level of WLC experienced by IT personnel evolved in the focal division of GLOBCOM, in the context of its offshore initiative. We label these temporally shifting patterns of the relationship or "stages" as Initiation, Distribution, Delegation, and Separation (see Table 4.1).

The Baseline Stage

Baseline represents the state that organizations such as the division of GLOBCOM we studied find themselves in, prior to their decision to create offshore development centers (ODCs). In such arrangements, users/clients of application systems are colocated with the design/development team, or, at the minimum, exist within the same larger geographical location (e.g., country), thereby minimizing the complications that time, space, and cultural distances pose to the ISD processes. ISD projects, in such situations, are undertaken by a team

Table 4.1 Evolving offshoring operational practices in B2B division of GLOBCOM

Stage of offshoring→	*Baseline stage*	*Initiation stage*	*Distribution stage*	*Delegation stage*	*Separation stage*
WLC onshore	Escalating out of control, because of ever-increasing workload	Somewhat greater than earlier, because of added responsibility to bringing offshore personnel up to speed; expectations of reduced WLC (Work–Life Conflict) due to offshoring	Very high, especially for key onshore personnel	Reduced from levels at earlier stage	Reverts to approximately baseline level
WLC offshore	NA	High for relocated offshore personnel; not applicable for new hires at offshore	High for all personnel, particularly high for women	Alarmingly high	Reduced to a level considered approximately at par for IT professionals in the country (still higher than onshore)
Offshore–onshore configuration	NA (no offshore)	Offshore as a *subordinate extension* of onshore	Offshore as a *collaborative partner* of onshore	Offshore as a *services provider* for onshore (operating with minimal involvement of onshore)	*Federated*, with offshore dealing autonomously with client

Stage of offshoring→	*Baseline stage*	*Initiation stage*	*Distribution stage*	*Delegation stage*	*Separation stage*
Nature of onshore–offshore identity	*Local identity*	*Differentiated Identity*	*Integrated Identity*	*Fragmented Identity*	*Pseudo-autonomous local entities*
Nature of ISD task allocation (across offshore and onshore)	*Local*	*Low interdependency; low complexity*	*High interdependency* across locations; "Follow the sun" based task allocation	*Low interdependency desired by onshore, often this was not realized* *High dependency of offshore on onshore*	*Localized in certain cases* based on IS platform architecture and client relationship with offshore
Evolution of assumptions about WLC	Improvement of WLC an imperative for onshore personnel's well-being and for prevention of turnover of key personnel	WLC can be reduced through allocation of work, to offshore development center	Optimism about reduced WLC replaced by a realization onshore that current work practices are stressful and have negative impact on WLC; offshore willing and able to absorb the challenges to WLB	Reduced extent of communication and communication synchronicity reduces WLC	Organizational well-being affected by differential WLB across organizational units; Local (onshore) interests should not drive WLB considerations and offshoring relationships

of co-located (or proximally located) individuals with strong relational ties among themselves as well as with the clients, who have the opportunity to interact as and when necessary, thereby making coordination relatively easy. In some situations, the organization may engage in traditional onshore outsourcing, where a portion of the systems development efforts is shifted to third-party vendors who may also be co-located, or be situated within the borders of the same country.

WLC Issues in the Baseline Stage

The work–life balance issues faced by IT organizations in such situations are quite similar to (other) organizations operating in the current hypercompetitive economy, irrespective of the tasks involved. As Felstead et al. (2002) suggest, with the increasing intensification of work and the constant productivity pressures faced by organizations, employees experience rapid escalations in WLCs. Quesenberry et al., (2006, p. 37) note that *IT workers* face even stronger WLC challenges, owing to the incessant changes in the technological environments, constant project deadlines, and shorter job tenure of employees within organizations, which, in turn, forces the employees to continuously adjust to new organizational cultures and environments. Some tactics used by organizations to manage work–life balance issues in such a stage are discussed below.

Empathy and "Afternoons in the Park"

Social adaptation theory suggests that organizations recognize and make sense of the changing world, and "respond to societal norms and expectations" (Felstead et al., 2002). Consistent with this perspective, companies tend to respond to the emerging work–life balance challenges by introducing practices to mitigate them. In GLOBCOM, we found a number of practices being used to ease some of the pressures that employees experienced on a daily basis. One specific "response" was the development of a "morale committee" that investigated, developed, and implemented several programs for increasing employees' "motivation and morale." Such initiatives included appointing empathetic managers who would keep an open communication channel, and reiterating to employees the organizational management's appreciation of the employees' dedicated efforts. For example, one of the managers in GLOBCOM mentioned the following:

> I think being more open with communication helps to keep the motivation and morale up... [Saying] "I know you guys had to work the weekend...and I know that sucks...[but] there is a light at the end of the tunnel, and I really do appreciate the work the team is doing to make sure we meet these milestones.

Other tactics directed toward addressing work-life conflict especially involved meeting as a group "in a restaurant or some other miniature golf event," or planning "afternoons in the park," thus enabling employees to take some time off during a workday and enjoy it with their families:

> So...we are all having an afternoon at the park. We are inviting families and so some of those things are planned for to help keep that morale up, and I feel those are important.

As discussed above, the "right" kind of manager can have a significant effect on improving the work–life balance of employees. For example, another manager mentioned:

> I think [GLOBCOM] historically has rewarded people who are very technically competent and have delivered key projects or key pieces of software in the past. Those people aren't always the best people-managers. We don't put enough emphasis on that as a skill. We need people who are leaders, who care about both your work-success and your life outside of work. ...who set realistic priorities and understand you are going to be most effective as an employee when you achieve a good work–life balance... I think that would improve morale a lot if I have to take a 7am call and a 9 pm call ...my manager's right there with me backing me up...

In other words, managing WLC in this stage is no different from what good managers in many organizations strive to achieve: improve and maintain high levels of motivation and morale by being empathetic, working in the trenches with employees who constantly face work–life balance challenges, and organizing social functions (if possible, within traditional work hours, and/or with families involved when appropriate), for the team to rejuvenate or to celebrate milestones.

The Initiation Stage

This stage involves the move toward the creation of offshore development centers (ODCs). Davis et al. (2006, p. 778), drawing on the logic of international economics, argued that the "cost factor" remained "one of the most critical practical arguments for offshoring put forward by companies." They also contended that firms had discovered that "offshoring benefits everyone—job seekers, stockholders, client firms, [and] vendors" financially, and many organizations use this justification as a basis for setting up such centers overseas. As organizations begin to shift work offshore, many realized that "cost efficiencies" along with "quality, and eventually delivery time" of work may be improved (Davis et al., 2006, p. 778). Motivated by similar factors, the B2B division of GLOBCOM too initiated efforts toward starting up ODCs in 2002. In addition to the above reasons, GLOBCOM's decision to engage in *offshore insourcing* was also triggered by the realization that shifting workload overseas would enable employees in the US offices to handle *more* projects at *lower costs*, and also help address some of their WLC concerns arising from their ever-increasing workload. As a senior GLOBCOM manager suggested: "We have to be able to work smarter, not just harder and more hours... that's not the answer." Offshoring was seen as a way to work "smarter" since more work could potentially be completed per dollar amount. According to another manager, shifting some of the work offshore not only meant sharing the workload, but also a sign that the organization was positioning itself for "global competition."

Whatever the motivation behind the development of the offshore organization, the initiation stage can be characterized by the following activities: managers/key personnel from the headquarters travel to the offshore sites (from the United States to India in this case) to set up operations at the remote centers. This involves, among other tasks, acquiring the physical premises for the offices, ensuring that appropriate technological infrastructure was available at the offshore site, and most importantly, hiring and training suitable employees. In the case of GLOBCOM, as the offshore site became functional, initially only simple systems development tasks could be assigned to the employees offshore in order to build confidence in this new mode of working. Not unexpectedly, the initiation of a development center overseas did not solve the WLC challenges for some of the stakeholders involved, and we discuss these in further detail below.

WLC Issues in the Initiation Stage

WLC of Management Staff Temporary Relocated to Offshore Location

The GLOBCOM managers who travelled from the headquarters to the offshore centers experienced a number of WLC challenges. Not only were they away from their personal/professional networks in the United States for an extended duration of time, simultaneously having to deal with the *challenges of cultural adaptation, but they also experienced the difficulties in hiring and retaining capable employees, as well as training them* on the application/systems environment and work practices of GLOBCOM. They also realized that *much of the WLC of working offshore resulted from receiving incomplete information about the system requirements from the onshore* location. This was the case even though these individuals (i.e., managers who temporarily relocated to India) had strong preexisting ties with key team members, other managers, and client representatives in the United States. One of the managers described the experiences during this period:

> I relocated to India in 2002 to set up the development organization... The stress we went through the first 2 years was enormous. Everybody put in like 60 hours including the weekends in the first year, because we didn't have many people...the people we hired in India were local, and they needed to be brought up to speed on the function and the business process and the way we do things... like [how] we release it to system testing from user-acceptance to finally production was all new to them... So, the few people who relocated from here [US, onshore] to there [India, offshore] really worked a lot of hours. A lot of stress. What makes it more complicated was when you got information that was not full...[at the offshore location].

Another manager noted:

> ...one of the frustrations for me is that there is such a high turnover, over in [India city] is difficult and we've seen challenges in hiring quality people and then retaining those people once we get them trained...

Alienating Part of the Onshore Workforce

While the individuals from GLOBCOM's US headquarters who were deployed offshore to set up the ODC were experiencing high WLC, their US-based (onshore) team members were optimistic that their WLC would experience a reduction due to the possibility of shifting some of their workload to offshore colleagues. Fortunately, with the amount of work that needed to be accomplished, there appeared little (if any) concern among GLOBCOM employees about their positions being shipped overseas, a common fear associated with offshoring. However, for some employees, especially those located in a secondary US location of GLOBCOM, the amount of resources being dedicated to developing sophisticated centers at the offshore sites, led to an "identity-crisis" and feelings of abandonment, adding significantly to strain. One GLOBCOM employee, who had earlier worked in one of GLOBCOM's secondary offices in the US, puts these feelings into words:

> India's got this big beautiful campus, and they built them a permanent building. Um, the [secondary US] facility has been there for 8/9 years and they [i.e., the employees] are still in temporary buildings, and [we were told]...you know...this was temporary and we were going to see how it worked out. Well, it's been 9 years... So [for employees in the secondary US sites] it's that perception of being the lesser. You're not investing in me, but you are investing in the Indian campus [on] like day 1.

Acknowledging That IT Profession Demands WLC Trade-Offs

Interestingly, the new employees at the Indian offshore development center during the initiation stage perceived minimal WLC. Apart from being situated on a beautiful new campus, the fact that they were working for this great global company, made them overlook the negatives, at least initially. Moreover, the type of tasks that they were involved in during this time were "simple enhancements" or "testing assignments," and as a result, did not cause any particular WLC that was beyond the norm in the IT profession. In the words of one GLOBCOM offshore manager:

> ...irrespective of where my team is located, even if my team is located where I am, I would still do long hours, not because it's distributed... It would happen otherwise also. IT is not a 9-5 job. If someone wants to work 9-5, then IT might not be the right place for them, certainly application development would not be the right place...

The Distribution Stage

Transition to this stage occurred after the ODC had been successfully set up, and some degree of stability had been achieved in the offshore organization in terms of human resources and work processes. Work was now accomplished through frequent communication/coordination between the offshore and onshore locations. GLOBCOM used a variety of different tactics for distributing work across these two locations. In certain cases, as one manager noted, they distributed the software development related tasks as follows:

> [we undertake]...certain pieces of work on-site [US] which is where the clients are located, and then we will...take it back to India. Get remainder of the work done...bring it back to the client, have [them] test it and run it....

In other cases, the team worked collaboratively on all phases of the project, taking advantage of the time differences among locations. A manager described this mode as follows:

> ...there are cases that the team is working on the same piece of work and they transition from one team to another. So, there's a person working in [US City] on the on-site location and working on the same piece of code and you have developers working in India which is off-shore, working on the same piece of code.

In such cases, the individuals in the two locations need to "... work hand in hand. They are like shadows of each other."

WLC Issues in the Distribution Stage

While the purpose of distributed work was to take advantage of the low-cost human resources, shift workload to development staff offshore, and derive advantages from round-the-clock development (also referred to as "follow-the-sun approach"), it was evident to GLOBCOM's B2B division management that the pressures of working with colleagues across time and space was beginning to raise the WLC of employees in both locations, and was negatively affecting their sense of well-being. In the context of knowledge work such as IS development, this could well translate to a reduction of the efficiency and effectiveness of the software development projects. Moreover, with the tight labor markets for talented and qualified staff both in the United States and India, it was imperative for the company to address the WLC issues in a meaningful way. Below, we discuss these issues in further detail.

Coordination Difficulties Across Onshore and Offshore Locations

The difficulties in coordination among onshore and offshore team members, that were required for seamlessly transferring tasks from one location to another, was seen *as a key source of frustration.* One manager reflected:

> The coordination required to pull [everyone] together and really achieve all these code changes on a short timeline was incredible....

To mitigate these above-mentioned coordination-related challenges, the software development team members tried out different work arrangements (e.g., working different shifts to match the time zones in India). One member provided the following account of such a work practice in GLOBCOM:

> But what you can do is accommodate ... for example, I could have every Wednesday be a noon-midnight or be a midnight-noon day, rather than be an 8-5. ... Yes, I did that on purpose, but by working two shifts -- a regular shift during the week and one day where I am on this really wildly absurd shift, maybe it's a 2 am-noon -- It allows me to work 40 hours but then work on a schedule which allows me to communicate rapidly and frequently so I could set all the meetings up between 2 am and 8 am my time and actually have a pretty solid hit with my developers in India. ... Most of the developers in India will work until 8:30 on a certain day if you ask them to and if you set it up so your leads are doing that at the same time, so that, for example, on my day where I am working 2am-noon is the same day where the lead in India is working from 2:30pm-midnight... It is odd hours...but we have an entire 10 hour day where I...IM him anytime and we can chat.

Such a work practice *to ensure synchronicity of communications and synchronous virtual presence across geographical and temporal boundaries* is not unknown in the literature or in practice, and was initially viewed by GLOBCOM as an effective means of mitigating coordination problems; however, it was soon discovered that *such an arrangement is hard to sustain over a long period of time* (e.g., the entire duration of a large software development project). A manager described the difficulties posed by the need to coordinate activities in the two locations (United States and India) through teleconference meetings in the following quote:

> Sometimes [there were meetings] early morning and late night... Team 1 in the morning, and Team 2 in the evening, right. It kills people... It kills people on both ends, it's not just a [US city] problem, it is an India problem too.

Another manager noted:

> The other thing I personally have a pet-peeve with is we don't have kind of official best practices on when to have meetings... We'll get requests for 6:30 am meetings the same day we get requests for 9 pm meetings... it's wrong...you feel terrible saying no to either one because you know it's going to impede the progress of the project.

Lack of Requisite Knowledge and Process Maturity Offshore
The coordination-related problems arose not only because of the lack of colocation among the employees in the US and the India sites, but more so because of the huge differences in the time zones of the two countries, which affected their ability to get quick answers whenever clarification on a particular issue was required. The Indian employees, owing to their shorter tenure within GLOBCOM, *needed* to acquire knowledge on a daily basis, and required "answers" and clarifications from their US-based counterparts frequently. This caused frustrations and strain not only for the Indian employees, but also for the US-based employees. One of the US-based managers noted:

> if people don't become knowledgeable, [for] anything and everything ...they have to ask me a question, I can only do some much in a day. I can only work 16/17 hours in a day. ... So. I become the bottleneck. There have been situations that have happened...Everything [offshore] was dependent on me.

The solution, in the words of another "stretched" manager in the United States, was: "They [i.e., the offshore personnel] have to learn, they have to learn, they have to learn." Some offshore employees attempted to work around late night telephone meetings with their US counterparts by relying more heavily on alternate communication tools such as email. However, email, owing to its asynchronous nature, often resulted in delayed (or inaccurate) responses to their queries. A GLOBCOM developer in the United States expressed dissatisfaction with the use of email as a communication tool between the two sites during the distribution stage, when it was critical for the Indian development team members to "catch-up," and acquire the knowledge necessary for completing the software development tasks assigned to them:

> E-mail communication works ok, but then again…if you write a paragraph, like a 5- or 6- line paragraph, have 6 people read it, you will get 6 different answers. Similarly, they write an e-mail, you are sure what he/she is asking for, so you send a reply and they figure out that no, no, no…you meant something else …

In other words, it was not easy for GLOBCOM members, involved in intensive knowledge work in the form of systems development, to substitute synchronous meetings with asynchronous communication.

Balancing the Interests of Onshore and Offshore Workers

Existing literature suggests that one of the reasons why organizations opt for offshore insourcing as opposed to offshore outsourcing is that, in an insourcing arrangement, organizations would be able to protect their intellectual property, prevent knowledge spillovers to competitors, and most importantly, reduce problems related to differences in organizational culture (since in the case of insourcing, employees in the onshore as well as offshore centers would be part of the same organization and thus a similar organizational culture). While these advantages exist in insourcing, the case of GLOBCOM alerted us to potential pitfalls associated with the WLC of employees which organizations need to be aware of. In an insourcing situation, the organization needs to pay attention to the WLC concerns of not only its onshore employees but also of its offshore center employees; in the case of outsourcing to vendors based overseas, the (offshore) workers' well-being remains the responsibility of the third-party offshore vendor, and thus the organization can focus on developing ways to minimize its (onshore) employees' WLC, sometimes by transferring the onshore employees' conflicts to the offshore location. Paying attention to WLC issues on both sides (i.e., onshore and offshore) simultaneously is clearly more challenging. Moreover, for organizations undertaking offshore insourcing, a realization about the need to balance work and life of offshore employees takes time and reflection—after all, offshoring was conceived in the first place as an *instrumental tactic* to achieve large gains in productivity from the onshore perspective (e.g., Robinson & Kalakota, 2004).

The Offshore Perspective: The Roles of Infrastructure and Culture

Staff in the offshore development centers, owing to their shorter tenure, realized that they needed to spend much more effort and time in "learning the tricks of the game," and to take the brunt of the pressure and uncertainty associated with distributed work—this contributed to WLC. A US-based employee expressed empathy for the difficulties faced by the offshore staff:

> I would say there is more stress in the other side of the water...like in India. Because you know, we started this operation about 4-4.5 years ago, even now, there is really [no] ... process maturity.

Often these problems in GLOBCOM's offshore development centers in India could be attributed to *a lack of symmetry in technological infrastructure,* which forced the Indian employees to work (and stay) at the office for longer durations at a stretch in an effort to coordinate and "sync" with their counterparts in the United States. According to a US-based manager, offshore employees have fewer choices in trying to deal with the imbalance:

> It is not that easy for them to do that, calling [the US] from home because it's an international call. Right? The price is...you can look at that factor too. Commute is a problem. You hear that it's not, but that it is because the office is a little bit away from the city and that is a problem to some. The work–life balance problem is on both ends. It's here and it's there. For here, there are certain things/ways that we can mitigate it. There, there's no other choice for them... They have to be in the office most of the time.

The problem may have been even greater for the women employees in India, many of whom, due to cultural norms, were not expected to be out working late (This societal norm is no doubt changing). For the sake of their careers, and pride in their professionalism, many of them *did* stay late at the office when required, often causing strains in their traditional family structures, and resulting in role conflicts and emotional distress. Further, the safety of women (or for that matter, men) returning home late at night could not be taken for granted. Companies such as GLOBCOM had to take necessary measures to lessen these conflicts faced by their workforce in the offshore location, and to ensure their security. A US-based manager who had visited the offshore site explained:

> ... you are asking them to work late and you better make sure they have transportation to reach their home late at night especially when it comes to women because again ... [their] society is not really supportive of women working late. Yeah, so I have seen a lot of people struggling. They come up with some arrangements, but you know... at the end of the day, task is given to them, they have to finish, so that's another stress for... working women.

An India-based GLOBCOM manager, however, strongly maintained that balancing work and life wasn't really that difficult for team members based in India. The manager then went on to explain how offshore workers balance their work and personal lives:

> I do not [participate in] very large personal life activities during the week. My family, relatives, everyone knows. They know weekends are the best... I never plan...and my team never plans...to work over weekends, and our weekend starts on Friday evening. Friday evening, I am gone, my team is gone... If anyone has to come and work, they need to get my approval... So, people would schedule social events, dinner with me over the weekend and not during the week, unless...there's no way out, then I could still make time. That's called balancing.

Managing Expectations About the IT Profession

Another US-based GLOBCOM manager offered an alternate solution for dealing with the WLC issues of the employees at the two sites. He argued that it was not just sufficient to work late or start early. To deal with these problems, one had to change his/her expectation regarding one's work patterns:

> ...I think [the conflict between work and life] is unavoidable if your expectation is that you'll only work between 8 and 5. I think your expectation has to bend to world time. ...I think you really only have those two choices

> though. I don't think you have the choice, I am going to work between 8-5 and I am going to force this system to meet my needs. The sun isn't going to listen and you know...if all you are doing is by forcing the cohort on the other side of the planet to be up your hours...between 8pm-5am, you've lowered his productivity.

Another US-based manager said rather definitively:

> ...work-life balance is an odd thing. You have to change your expectations to be on world time.

No Simple Approach

Over time, a realization emerged that none of the tactics used was going to be sufficient for easing WLC concerns of GLOBCOM's onshore as well as offshore employees.. *Changing expectations regarding the developers' or managers' working hours, making members in the different distributed locations work on different shifts in an effort to "sync" their times, enabling employees to work from home, and other similar tactics were found to be only marginally effective.* While staggering work hours and rotating shifts to partially align the onshore and offshore times may help in mitigating time-related stresses from a *physiological stand point*, such synching alienated employees from their "social" clocks, which structure their family's and friends' activities around them (Sarker & Sahay, 2004). In addition, the lack of symmetry in technology availability between the onshore and offshore and locations posed additional challenges. Further, even untethered technologies (laptops) could not be easily transferred from one social context (workplace) to another (home):

> [Here] everyone has a laptop, everyone has a DSL to connect, which is still not available in India today, so we have several issues there...[Moreover] when you go home, you have other responsibilities to take care of.

Not finding any tactical solution to address challenges related to work–life balance issues, GLOBCOM started exploring possible changes in the nature of distribution of software development tasks between the on-site and offshore locations. Many US-based managers and technical staff in GLOBCOM had reached the point where they saw the need to *seriously reconsider their philosophy of working "hand-in-hand" with members of their Indian offshore center*, and decided to explore alternate strategies. This prompted the transition of the organization from the "distribution" stage to "delegation."

The Delegation Stage

This stage may be characterized as the shifting of software development project tasks to an offshore location (i.e., India, in the case of GLOBCOM) where offshore team(s) would be "responsible" for executing the entire project independently, instead of closely collaborating with their onshore (i.e., GLOBCOM United States) counterparts on every aspect of the project. A manager described this work arrangement and the underlying rationale:

> If you mix people in a particular project, they have to keep in sync. The only way to keep in sync is again… late night or early morning, right? So, what we are attempting to do is to try to cut the link. Very, very, very few projects...will have a mix of people from [Indian city] and in [US city]. For the majority of projects, it will be purely [US city] resource, or purely Indian resource.

The idea behind such a distribution of work was to make Indian staff "own" a project from start to finish, as described below:

> We've kinda babysat India up until this point. Um, and so going forward we are going to switch the models in that we're currently working on a lot of projects that are crossed through. Some part's done in India, some part's done in [US City]…. Well, that's not to say that we are throwing India into the deep-end of the pool, and if they can't figure out [the requirements], too bad for them. It just means that you have to work it out. This is your accountability.

This individual also provided the following "analogy[2]" of the current work distribution among the onshore and offshore development centers and the nature of distribution in the delegation stage:

> It's almost like my analogy with being with little kids…I try to tie my own shoe and the first few times I can't and then I just get frustrated, and

[2] In this analogy, the interviewee likens offshore staff to "little kids" and onshore managers to "mom.".

> then someone [like] Mom will show up and tie my shoe for me...whereas eventually [if] Mom said, 'I am not tying your shoes anymore. You can walk around with them untied or get some Velcro-closures...' I learned to tie my shoe because I didn't want to walk around with my shoes untied, and they didn't have Velcro shoes... And so, you...have to know when to let go.

The rationale behind such delegation was that transferring the responsibility (and therefore, the accountability) of the entire project to the offshore center would enable the offshore team to conduct ISD activities, without needing day-to-day clarifications from their US-based counterparts. Such a move was expected to ease some of the WLC experienced during the distribution stage.

Interestingly, while there was a distinct push to make offshore responsible and accountable, there appeared to be a desire among onshore personnel to hold on to the control of the projects, albeit in a subtle manner. A manager explained:

> I think that the challenge [for the US-based group] [to] be maintaining a level of control to know what they [offshore team-members] are doing without controlling what they do.

Given the nature of business of GLOBCOM, the clients for B2B Division's systems development projects would still be located in the United States, enjoying copresence, shared contexts, and historically close linkages with managers in B2B division's headquarters (onshore). Because the communication linkages between the offshore site and the client representatives were not sufficiently developed, the US-based onshore managers of B2B division remained the nerve centers for client-related information and system requirements, and the envisaged model of offshore location "owning" a system in its entirety was not easy to bring to fruition. To gain an assessment of the effectiveness of delegation, onshore leadership considered implementing a tracking system (e.g., by logging the number of queries/phone calls from offshore to onshore employees). As the senior staff manager said:

> If [a particular onshore employee] is getting 22 phone calls per day every day for a month [from offshore], then we haven't solved anything....

While the initial trends appeared to be promising in many project teams, especially from the onshore perspective, there was still a long way to achieving goals of delegation in the other teams.

WLC Issues in the Delegation Stage

The initiative for enabling the offshore team in India to take the responsibility for entire software development projects was at least partially triggered by the persisting WLC problems on *both* sides of the offshoring dyad, but primarily voiced by the onshore members. We next discuss the consequences of the work arrangement in the delegation stage.

Onshore Balance at the Expense of Offshore?

The increased accountability and "independence" of the Indian ODCs started moving the organization in a direction where the WLC of US-based onshore employees started to improve. However, for the employees based offshore, in India, things appeared to be taking a different turn. Indeed, if one were to consider the aggregate WLC of the organization as a whole, it would appear that the offshore employees' increasing WLC more than compensated for the improvement in the WLC for onshore staff. One of the reasons for the increased WLC of the employees at the offshore center is the fact that, within this arrangement designed to increase their accountability, the control in terms of receiving/clarifying systems requirements (and possibly critical elements of the budget) was still retained at the US headquarters. Also, given the geographical location of the clients (in the United States), and the fact that the clients' relational ties were still closer with application managers located in onshore, and that it was unlikely that these ties would shift overnight to the managers in the offshore location, obtaining clarifications about the requirements, the political contexts, and information about how things "really" worked, was very difficult for the offshore managers and staff.

Requirements for Independence: Communication Networks, Application Knowledge, and Control

For the offshore-based team members, the transition from receiving information on a "need-to-know basis" to a mode of working where they are having to take charge of acquiring and managing the entire information related to an application, drastically increased their strain and demands on time. A GLOBCOM member in the United States empathized with the situation of the Indian members.

> It would be very difficult [for the Indian members], because the flow of information is from here always. Because our business team sits here. Our information comes from our business team. Our business is here, in [US City], ...our...other groups within [GLOBCOM], we are...pretty much here...it is like most of the business information is available [in the US.] It can go only one way. So, it would be very difficult if they want to control this from India tomorrow. I would say India has more of the receiving end on this in terms of information and the delivery will be flowing back from there to here.

Further, the level of maturity of the offshore employees, not only with respect to the knowledge about the clients and their requirements, but also regarding the understanding of GLOBCOM's work practices, had not become at par with that of their onshore counterparts. This conflict in knowledge often created challenges for them in terms of performing their tasks independently without the continuous "babysitting" by key onshore developers and project managers. One of our US-based respondents reflected on this issue:

> We kind of tell them...the problem. [We] don't tell them this is the context [within which] the decision was taken...what other scenarios did we address and why... We just communicate this is the decision that was taken, so [they] kinda feel left out...since[they] didn't know what happened, [they] only knew that was the decision taken here.

One other WLC issue that the offshore employees reported experiencing in GLOBCOM during this phase pertains to the delays in getting appropriate responses from their onshore counterparts. Given that the offshore employees were being expected to take up more responsibility, and to work independently without being "spoon-fed" by the onshore development leads/managers, key onshore members did not see the need (or the obligation) to be available early mornings and late nights to answer questions, or to provide clarifications to their offshore counterparts as a priority. While this may be interpreted as leading to a significantly reduced level of WLC for the onshore members, for the offshore members, who need the answers urgently (due to their incomplete knowledge and the lack of necessary connections to elicit nuanced application-related information from clients), this meant that they either had to stay up late to synchronize with the time zones of the US offices (seriously hindering their own WLB), or seek out alternate asynchronous communication media such as email (which often proved ineffective). A US-based employee could relate to the stress of the Indian employees when relying on email, given their limitations in the required knowledge:

> If you are lucky, it can get answered in a day or two, if it is not, it's going to take a longer period of time. So, the work-life challenge is that the knowledge is really, really important.

Work with Few Dependencies

One tactic that was easing the pressure arising from the delays was to distribute *work that had few* "dependencies" across the locations. The budget for these centers was still controlled by the US headquarters, but the shipment of independent work would ensure the need for less coordination between the two locations, and less reliance on the center colocated with the client for information/clarification. A GLOBCOM developer alluded to this strategy in the following quote:

> Um...I would say independent work needs to be identified... Identify the work which has a less dependency. More details, less dependent on other people. So that kind of work you deliver it to India, that can be...we have very smart people there. They can deliver really, really fast. When you start with the dependencies on people here...that's when they, at the same time, like when something is dependent from here to India, that's a lot of communication issues happens and chaos and delays and stuff like that.

Such independent work could involve the development of a new, generic application system (not customized for a particular client), and therefore could be developed with minimal (or no) interaction with the client (or business analysts colocated with the client). Reduction in such coordination would help in reducing the WLCs related to working in distributed environments, and potentially improve job and personal life outcomes for all parties involved.

Equitable Policies

Apart from the work itself, certain questions related to the equity between the onshore and offshore staff would need to be reconsidered, if the offshore organization was to be considered capable to undertake projects independently. In terms of their "identity," the offshore employees needed to feel like *equal* members of a global organization, not like "stepchildren" of a US organization. An onshore manager elaborated on this issue:

> I see inequities across the board, and you know some of that comes from [the fact that] we do work in India because it is very cost-effective. We don't necessarily do it because that's where the most-skilled individuals are, although sometimes it is [the case]... You know...one [disparity] I recently uncovered, when I tried to fly of my team-members from [India-City] over here. Our policy [for US-based employees] is typically...you book business class if you are on a longer flight. That doesn't apply from them...oh no, no, now we have a special policy [for offshore employees]. We need to save money here. Why is that? ...policy-wise, facility-wise, support, um...we should try to make those situations as equal as possible.

Not surprisingly, an offshore manager also indicated displeasure about such inequities.

Clearly, for offshore employees to develop ownership of the organization's work and identity, equitable policies are an imperative. Indeed, it may be argued that HR policies and privileges of offshore employees in the delegation stage need to evolve *toward* globally equitable standards *from* the onshore headquarters-centric policies—these may have been appropriate in the earlier stages of the insourcing relationship (i.e., baseline and initiation). In the absence of globally equitable policies, the work-life conflict of offshore employees is likely to go up. This is because the expectations of equal productivity and accountability of offshore employees are not perceived to be fair or balanced without providing them with a comparable degree of control or status in the organization.

The above discussion highlights that, while the transition to the "delegation" stage may have been intended to ease the problems related to WLC of GLOBCOM's employees, in reality, it helped manage the WLC levels of *only* the US-based (i.e., onshore) employees. Given the insourcing context, GLOBCOM, a premier *global* company, needed to deal with the WLC issue, not only as balancing *work* and *life* of its US-based (i.e., *onshore*) employees, but also balancing the needs and privileges of its *offshore* employees. While we recognize that dealing with WLC issues on both ends of a dyad (separated by about a 12-hour time difference, lack in parity in knowledge-levels, in different economic/cultural settings, etc.) is challenging, we believe that this issue is worth reflecting upon. Some of the ideas discussed within the "separation" stage may be helpful in this regard.

The Separation Stage

While there has not been any explicit discussion surrounding a transition to this stage when our relationship with B2B division with GLOBCOM ended, parts of GLOBCOM appeared to be moving in the direction described in this stage, wherein the onshore and offshore units were configured as a federated organization, with the offshore and onshore units operating as autonomous business units. Of course, such separation can only be attained through strategic (and not tactical) decision-making in the company. In the "separation stage," not only would the offshore unit be responsible for "owning" each project, but it would also be responsible for generating its own resources, and garnering as well as serving its *own* set of clients. Carmel and Agarwal (2002) alluded to this practice, among firms that adopt a "pro-active strategic focus" to offshoring. In addition, Carmel and Agarwal argued that firms that initiated the setup of such independent centers, expected the centers "to develop new IT products or systems, take ownership of entire IT systems and software products, and assume responsibility for end-to-end systems" (p. 71). The clients, in such cases, tend to be more local, situated within the same geographical region, national border, and/or time zone.[3] Such a change in GLOBCOM (specifically, its B2B division) would inherently decrease offshore employees' reliance on their onshore counterparts for client-related information. Further, since the members in the offshore development centers would be responsible for "the entire lifecycle- from requirements gathering through implementation and support" (Carmel & Agarwal, 2002, p. 71), there would be less need for coordination and synchronization between the two locations. In the separation stage, if clients were to be located in the United States and away from the offshore development team, a dedicated "bridge organization," potentially located in the United States, *but accountable to and under the control of the offshore units*, would be used. Such an arrangement is likely to help manage the WLC. A US-based manager explained:

> ... the offshore team [have] their own areas of responsibilities on the platform... They may own a core piece of platform that they are responsible

[3] Naturally, for this to happen, India would need to develop further economically, and become a hub for overseas operations of B2B division's clients.

for, and their only reliance [on onshore] is potentially using data from other parts of the platform.

An India-based manager (from a different division) alluded to another approach to separation. In some cases, the trust developed between the client and the offshore team as a result of successful project deliveries over a period of time, catalyzed the transfer of the entire project operations (including client relationship management) to offshore. In the words of this manager:

> ...there are some scenarios where separation...actually happens. Some customers, especially those, which had positive experience with offshore for a few years, have...they are saying – I do not want any North American presence on this project. I am comfortable with the entire thing being done from India...

The manager also added that in such situations, the transfer of project operations responsibilities drastically reduced WLC:

> Yes, it does [reduce WLC]. The number of calls we have with... customers is much less... customer calls are not that frequent, right? ... In these scenarios, definitely work-life balance [improves].

While these instances do provide some evidence regarding the success of the separation stage when it is implemented with careful forethought, such a transformation is not easy to effectively implement. In words of a manager:

> When the [offshoring] model has become really mature...then, you know, we see some cases [of separation]... Otherwise we are...in the distribution stage or the delegation stage.

Of course, it must be noted that the viability of using such a "separation" strategy for the offshore development center would depend a great deal on a variety of external factors such as the number of possible clients in a certain country, growth opportunities, costs, long-term organizational strategy, and so on. Given the limited feasibility of "separation" in many organizations, it is worth considering an alternative—that of "integration," by creating such unison in thinking that is independent of location (i.e., has "locational transparency") for the entire team. This would obviously take time and significant management commitment. Much of the WLC issues experienced in GLOBCOM originated from the lack of adequate knowledge of the offshore employees and the absence of a shared frame of reference between onshore and offshore personnel. Our view is that, with the passage of time, and with the right training and knowledge management approach as well as appropriate human resource practices to mitigate the loss of knowledge through turnover, the employees at the offshore development centers would match the strength of relational linkages with the clients as well as the domain expertise and other application-related knowledge of the onshore employees. This would enable the development/enactment of shared norms and interpretive schemes even when "projects that are crossed through" (as one GLOBCOM developer stated), thereby facilitating the seamless accomplishment of work without much coordination or process losses associated with temporal and spatial distances. However, such a seamless accomplishment of project tasks is challenging because it requires an alignment in task and social structure across members of the two locations (Sarker & Sahay, 2003). As mentioned above, serious efforts are needed to create this level of synergy in cognition and work practices. Table 4.2 provides a summary of the key WLC issues associated with the different stages.

Discussion

Through an interpretive case study of a division in a globally reputed organization, we have explored some of the WLC issues in the context of IT offshore insourcing. Our review of the literature suggests that to date much of the offshoring literature (whether on outsourcing or insourcing) has focused mostly on the issues of cost, availability, and skills of the individuals, and the risks associated with this practice. For example, Robinson and Kalakota (2004, p. 2) argue that offshoring "hinges on cost management through labor and skill arbitrage." Similarly, due to geopolitical instability and risks "to data security, data privacy, and intellectual property" (Patterson, 2006, p. 42), the assessment and management of the risk of offshore projects receives significant attention in the literature (Robinson & Kalakota, 2004, p. 236). What our case study highlights, however, is yet another critical piece of the offshoring "mystery," that of the WLC of the human resource involved in this practice (see Fig. 1). Surprisingly, this issue has received scant attention (if any) from researchers in the past.

Table 4.2 Key WLC issues associated with each stage

Stage	*WLC issues*
Baseline stage	Issues due to the overload and intensification of work that are experienced in virtually all contemporary organizations, especially in the IT sector. These issues exist independent of any offshoring decision
Initiation stage	Overall, optimism regarding WLC among onshore workers. There is however a need to allay the fears about onshore employee downsizing, and about the organization's priorities shifting overseas. Managers who are temporarily relocated offshore to manage the set up and initial operations of the Offshore Development Centers face severe WLC challenges; these challenges need to be addressed through formal organizational policies
Distribution stage	Issues arise on both offshore and onshore locations, primarily due to the lack of application-specific knowledge and process maturity offshore. There is a need for frequent synchronous meetings between offshore and onshore staff for clarifications, and given the time differences, results in burn-out and fatigue on both sides
Delegation stage	The arrangement sounds excellent in theory, though there are limitations in practice. First, there aren't (or weren't) many projects that can be made independent of onshore staff, and offshored. Second, without requisite knowledge and process maturity (which cannot be cultivated overnight), offshore employees in similar situations are unlikely to be able to handle the projects without seeking frequent clarifications, and without project management by offshore managers. Third, without offshore employees developing strong formal and informal linkages with clients located onshore, it is unlikely that they can execute a project independently without involving onshore staff, who are not expected to be available for providing clarifications to offshore staff. Thus, while onshore staff may experience lower WLC, for offshore staff, WLC can be expected to worsen significantly
Separation stage	Reverts back to local WLC issues associated with IT work, somewhat independent of the offshore insourcing relationship (as in the Baseline stage)

Domagalski (1999, p. 835) argues that traditionally, organizations have been viewed as "rationally driven enterprises," where "jobs could be designed for maximum productivity," and the "rational economic interests of the workers would prevail in their acceptance of scientific techniques." In such organizations, it was considered rational to overlook the socio-emotional needs of employees. However, in the last few years, the "emotional dimensions of the workplace" have begun to receive increasing attention (Domagalski, 1999, p. 833), and "the work/family balance is fast becoming the hot career issue of the new decade" (Caproni, 2004, p. 208). In light of this, we believe that the WLC issues of the workers should be at the center of focus in contexts such as offshoring of knowledge work, including but not limited to software development, where success of the initiative primarily rests on the human resources involved. As our study highlighted, much of the (positive) impacts which were expected to be in tune with the "rational interests of the workers" in GLOBCOM (e.g., working for one of the most highly regarded companies in the world, high salaries, superior technological infrastructure) were being dampened by the WLC concerns. While exemplary companies such as GLOBCOM are exploring ways to deal with WLC pressures associated with offshoring, the criticality of balancing is yet to be acknowledged in the literature, and is possibly not well understood in lesser companies. Some practical implications that emerge from our study include: a) implementing appropriate HR policies for onshore and offshore sites, b) structuring the relationship between onshore and offshore, keeping in mind the issues such as those of dependency and control, c) determining the nature of work to be assigned to offshore, and d) developing maturity, organizational knowledge sharing, and rich communication linkages of offshore locations with the primary onshore location and also the clients.

Our study further highlights that *WLC in the context of offshoring is not a monolithic concept, and is itself dynamic, evolving through (and partly driving) the various stages of the offshore insourcing relationship.* Much of the existing literature on WLB/WLC focuses on the development and implementation of several "family-friendly employment practices" (Felstead et al., 2002, p. 58). Several strategies such as enabling employees to work flexibly and to work from home/telecommuting, and providing generous maternity/paternity leaves have been suggested in an effort to improve the work–life balance of the employees, and to keep them satisfied and productive (Spinks, 2004). The underlying assumption behind this body of knowledge is that the *same set of temporally invariant tactics hold for managing WLC of organizational employees*, irrespective of their location. Our study, on the other hand, suggests that in the case of offshore insourcing, a *one-time implementation* of such tactics may not be the solution. The study suggests that relevant WLC-related antecedents continually change for the different stakeholders in offshore projects (please see Table 4.1), and it is important for organizations to continuously monitor these causes of WLC and their impacts, and rapidly implement tactics to counter emergent sources of imbalance.

Another point revealed by this study is that WLC is even more of a challenge in the context of offshore *insourcing*, owing to the fact that in insourcing, the offshore center is part of the global organization. This implies that offshore personnel can have an expectation of being accorded with equal status/privileges as their onshore counterparts. In other words, there is an implicit expectation that the company must strive to equitably manage WLC of *both* its onshore and offshore employees. Given the initial disparities between the onshore and offshore locations with respect to the levels of knowledge and experience of the personnel, control of the projects, location of the client, informal networks with key business people located in the US headquarters, etc., bringing about a balance in both sides of the dyad is no doubt challenging. For example, in the initiation stage, while the employees in India felt relatively low WLC, the managers from the United States who relocated to India for setting up offshore operations felt significant WLC. Also, the morale of the employees based (in a secondary location) in the United States suffered, leading to severe strain-based conflict when they learned of the huge amount of money being spent in developing state-of-the-art infrastructure in India, and this impact was largely unanticipated by GLOBCOM management, or at least, they did not show their sensitivity or understanding regarding this issue. We believe that in such situations it would be important to mitigate the strain of these US employees by involving them in "morale-boosting" activities, and emphasizing how the offshoring infrastructure in India would result in benefits for the downstream, and making conscious efforts to reduce their feelings of being treated as the "stepchild." In the distribution stage, where around-the-clock development was in full swing, and therefore the need for late night and early morning meetings, odd schedules, etc., there is significant WLC on both sides of the dyad. In such a stage, it is important to realize that such round-the-clock development is not feasible to sustain for a long duration of time, especially when the different locations do not have sufficient organizational and knowledge-related maturity. In such circumstances, one should only use the "follow-the-sun" approach if: (1) the tasks involved are simple, and require thin communication between the different locations, (2) it is a small project, and (3) for larger projects, task blocks with low interdependence can be allocated to different distributed locations (Sarker & Sahay, 2004). Some of the other WLC issues arising during this stage are due to the fact that members often have to participate in more than one meeting at "odd times" on the same day. We believe that being even-handed and considerate in scheduling these meetings, and staggering work times for different locations or switching work shifts for one location might help mitigate WLC concerns.

In the delegation stage, a different type of WLC challenge arises, necessitating the adoption of a different set of tactics to counterbalance it. In this phase, the WLC of the onshore employees lessens, but that of the offshore employees tends to increase dramatically. One of the reasons is that while they (offshore members) are now solely responsible for a project, they still need clarifications on a daily basis from their onshore counterparts. However, the onshore members (with the belief that work has now been fully delegated) may no longer feel the need to be available for providing information and clarifications at hours outside of their normal work schedule. This means that the offshore employees need to coordinate with the work times of the onshore employees, greatly increasing the work-life conflict they experience. We believe that in such situations, creating "bridge organizations," that is, a small group of onshore employees (appointed by rotation to minimize the duration of WLC on the employees) who would be available for clarifications at times outside of their regular work schedules could help mitigate this issue (e.g., Carmel & Agarwal, 2002). Further, having dashboard metrics in place for assessing the WLC concerns at each stage can also help identify these problems early, and can enable the organization to take prompt action before the problems escalate.

Finally, an unanticipated finding emerging from our study is that *WLC is not just a human resource problem, but can serve as a potent force that leads to a structural reconfiguration of an offshore insourcing relationship.* In GLOBCOM, for example, the decision to transition to the delegation stage, where the Indian center was made responsible for entire projects, was triggered in part by the severe WLC that employees faced prior to that stage. This finding further indicates the importance of WLC in the context of offshoring, and will hopefully encourage both researchers and practitioners to investigate this issue more closely.

Even though we have not used Border Theory (introduced in Chapter 1) to frame our case study, we feel that it is worth bringing the theory briefly into the discussion of the findings. The nature of the border in this case is multi-dimensional: it separates work and life for each of the employees and also separates offshore and onshore. The border crossers often have to deal with multiple aspects of the borders, and have very different experiences in border crossing between work and life, depending on which side of the offshore–onshore border they are in. Further, each day, employees cross not only the borders separating work and life, but also within their work borders, need to transcend the lines of demarcation between their own location and those of their remote colleagues (in terms of differences in culture, knowledge, time, to name only a few) (Sarker et al. 2018). The case revealed that border keepers do not appear to mind the borders in altogether neutral manner, demanding different levels of permeability and flexibility of the border for offshore and onshore locations. Yet, given that the offshore and onshore personnel exist within the same organizational border (GLOBCOM), and the insourcing context, questions about the fairness arise, when managers privilege onshore over offshore with respect to time, responsibilities, and control. The stages represent the different ways in which the borders get drawn and redrawn in the tussle to manage WLC of border crossers located onshore and offshore, with different implications for the crossers depending on which side of the border they are on.

We would like to emphasize that achieving a perfect balance in work/life in any context is challenging, more so in offshore insourcing situations, where employees have varied levels of knowledge, and are separated by significant time, distance, and cultural assumptions; yet, they need to "collaborate" seamlessly as if they are copresent. What can be done to ensure work–life balance in such situations? While this case provides some preliminary insights based on experiences of a globally renowned organization, scholars warn us that making the reduction of WLC an "overriding…goal" will force organizations to "over-plan…lives," as opposed to letting employees live lives, and thus "lead us down the same path that we are trying to get off" (Caproni, 2004, p. 213). While organizations must pay heed to the imbalance and its undesirable impacts, and continually strive to monitor and reduce these effects (Caproni, 2004, p. 214), forcing a balance with rigid policies (e.g., no work on weekends, no calls in the evenings, etc.) can be counterproductive, as the unintended consequence of such policies is often more WLC and stress. A process-based dynamic approach that is sensitive to the changing tensions and based on an empathetic understanding of colleagues'/subordinates' situations holds more promise. In the end, it needs to be acknowledged that in today's hypercompetitive distributed and global workplace, attaining the *ideal of balance* as an optimally desired state for each and every employee may be unattainable (Spinks, 2004). What really counts is the degree to which the management remains true to the values that can help minimize employees' WLC by designing task and work arrangements accordingly, and continues to strive to make the working conditions fit the needs of its employees.

Conclusion

In this chapter, we presented an in-depth case study that showed the changing nature of WLC in an offshoring relationship that not only had consequences for the individual onshore and offshore employees but also led to the repeated restructuring of the offshoring relationship.

In the next chapter, we move from an offshore insourcing, a specific organizational context, to a technological context, that of mobile technology used by IT professionals and the nature of impact it may have on them. A key point that emerges in this chapter and the next is that managing WLC is far more complex than isolating and, when possible, manipulating individual factors uncovered in Chapters 2 and 3.

References

Aron, R., Clemons, E. K., & Reddi, S. (2005). Just right outsourcing: Understanding and managing risk. *Journal of Management Information Systems, 22*(2), 37–55.

Caproni, P. J. (2004). Work/life balance: You can't get there from here. *The Journal of Applied Behavioral Science, 40*(2), 208–218.

Carmel, E., & Agarwal, R. (2002). The maturation of offshore sourcing of information technology work. *MIS Quarterly Executive, 1*(2), 65–86.

Davis, G. B., Ein-Dor, P., King, W. R., & Torkzadeh, R. (2006). IT offshoring: History, prospects and challenges. *Journal of the AIS, 7*(11), 770–795.

Domagalski, T. A. (1999). Emotion in organizations: Main currents. *Human Relations, 52*(6), 833–852.

Dutta, A., & Roy, R. (2005). Offshore outsourcing: A dynamic causal model of counteracting forces. *Journal of Management Information Systems, 22*(2), 15–35.

Felstead, A., Jewson, N., Phizacklea, A., & Walters, S. (2002). Opportunities to work at home in the context of work–life balance. *Human Resource Management Journal, 12*(1), 54–76.

Levy, D. L. (2005). Offshoring in the new global political economy. *Journal of Management Studies, 42*(3), 685–693.

Niederman, F., Kundu, S., & Salas, S. (2006). IT software development offshoring: A multi-level theoretical framework and research agenda. *Journal of Global Information Management, 14*(2), 52–74.

Patterson, D. A. (2006). Offshoring: Finally facts vs. folklore. *Communications of the ACM*, *49*(2), 41–42.

Quesenberry, J. L., Trauth, E. M., & Morgan, A. J. (2006). Understanding the 'mommy tracks': A framework for analyzing work–family balance in the IT workforce. *Information Resources Management Journal, 19*(2), 37–53.

Rao, M. T. (2004). Key issues for global IT sourcing: Country and individual factors. *Information Systems Management, 21*(3), 16–21.

Robinson, M., & Kalakota, R. (2004). *Offshore outsourcing: Business models*. Mivar Press.

Sakthivel, S. (2007). Managing risk in offshore systems development. *Communications of the ACM, 50*(4), 69–75.

Sarker, S., Ahuja, M., & Sarker, S. (2018). Work–life conflict of globally distributed software development personnel: An empirical investigation using border theory. *Information Systems Research, 29*(1), 103–126.

Sarker, S., & Sahay, S. (2004). Implications of space and time for distributed work: An interpretive study of US-Norwegian systems development teams. *European Journal of Information Systems, 13*(1), 3–20.

Sarker, S., & Sahay, S. (2003). Understanding virtual team development: An interpretive study. *Journal of the AIS, 4*(1), 1–38.

Sarker, S., Sarker, S., & Jessup, L. (2010). Interpreting a case of offshore insourcing: A work–life balance perspective. *Academy of Management Conference*.

Spinks, N. (2004). Work–life balance: Achievable goal or pipe dream? *The Journal for Quality and PArticipation, 27*(3), 5–11.

Walsham, G. (1995). Interpretive case studies in IS research: Nature and method. *European Journal of Information Systems, 4*, 74–81.

CHAPTER 5

Mobile Technologies and Work–Life Conflict

Mobile technologies are profoundly affecting both how work gets done and how we live our lives. In many sectors, there is an increasing need for ubiquitous access to systems and information, coordination with colleagues across time and space, and constant connectivity. While readily acknowledging the benefits of using mobile technologies in their professional lives, many mobile workers also express a sense of helplessness arising from the constant intrusion of these technologies into their personal lives.

In this chapter, we focus primarily on personal mobile technology use by knowledge workers, specifically IT professionals, and its impact on Work–Life Conflict (WLC). We first present some basic results from our survey data (see Chapter 2 for the description of the sample). Thereafter, we discuss, in detail, some of the findings from a qualitative study of mobile use and work–life conflict (see Appendix 1 for the interviewees who participated).

The qualitative study and its discussion presented in this chapter is a revised version of a published paper: Sarker, Suprateek, Xiao, Xiao, Sarker, Saonee, and Ahuja, Manju (2012). Managing Work-Life Balance of Mobile Technology-Enabled IT Workers: Perspectives and Strategies. *MIS Quarterly Executive*, pp. 143–157.

S. Sarker et al., *Navigating Work and Life Boundaries*,
https://doi.org/10.1007/978-3-030-72759-8_5

An Overview of Use Patterns and the Impact on Work–Life Conflict

Although there has been much research on the WLC challenges faced by workers and managers in traditional industries, research focusing on such challenges faced by knowledge workers such as IT professionals is sparse. With respect to the use of mobile technologies, the research to date has primarily focused on the positive effects of using mobile technologies for business. The most notable benefits summarized by Sarker et al. (2012) include:

- The potential for 24 × 7 uninterrupted connectivity to human as well as information resources
- Increased flexibility
- Improved coordination
- Increased productivity through flexibility in time management
- Pleasure and enjoyment
- Availability of multiple media and genres of communication suited for different scenarios.

Further, a recent study by Chatterjee et al. (2017) argued that mobile technologies offer affordances such as "mobility, connectedness, identifiability, interoperability, and personalization" (p. 1) that contribute to contemporary organizations' fluidity, a characteristic that has been seen as valuable for innovation, survival, and success of many organizations. With respect to our topic of interest, recent literature suggests that much like other information and communication technologies (ICTs), mobile technologies can afford flexibility for individuals thereby leading to reduced WLC; however, they also note that mobile technologies more often than not contribute significantly to higher WLC (Adisa et al., 2017; Middleton, 2008; Sarker et al., 2012). Our survey data (see Appendix 3) showed that among global software development professionals, the use of mobile technologies is generally associated with higher WLC. Specifically, based on a total of 1000 responses, we found increases in the following activities related to mobile technology increased WLC:

- the *proportion of job functions* an individual can accomplish using their mobile device
- the *number of minutes* an individual spends on a typical day on their mobile device

- the *frequency* of communication (number of times) using their mobile device, and
- the *volume* of communication (how much) using their mobile device.

The first item suggests that the higher the potential of mobile technologies to be used, the higher the WLC is likely to be. The last three items all point to the fact that increased communication through mobile devices generally heightens WLC. Additionally, an interesting and potentially valuable result related not just to mobile technologies but to all ICTs used to communicate with distributed team members, had to do with the *deleterious effects of synchronicity*. Specifically, we found that the higher the volume (or frequency) of *synchronous communication* (e.g., voice or video calls, and instant messaging with an expectation of immediate action and responsiveness) of an individual with distributed team members, the greater the undesirable impact on the individual's WLC. However, increasing the volume (or frequency) of *asynchronous communication* (e.g., text, voice mail, and email with no expectation of immediate response) did not appear to increase WLC. As we saw in the case study presented in the previous chapter, the effect of synchronous communication on WLC is to be expected, especially in a globally distributed environment involving complex knowledge work with task interdependence across locations. This effect is primarily because bridging of the time differences, especially in a globally distributed context, can seldom be done without a serious incursion into the personal time of individuals in at least one location.

While the overall patterns reported above may be interesting, we were curious to know how the patterns varied as it related to the country in which the individual IT professional was based, as well as their gender. Below, we summarize some of the patterns revealed.

1. For women (233 out of the 1000 respondents), the proportion of job functions enabled by mobile phone, the frequency, and the volume of communication was not related to the WLC they experienced. Interestingly, the number of minutes they reported was related.

2. For men (767 out of the 1000 respondents), the proportion of job functions enabled by mobile phone, number of minutes, frequency, and the volume of communication were all related to WLC.
3. For US and UK-based respondents (who were 500 and 251 respondents respectively out of the 1000 respondents), the proportion of job functions enabled by mobile phone, number of minutes, frequency (weak relationship in case of UK respondents), and the volume of communication were all related to WLC.
4. For respondents from India (who were 249 out of the 1000 respondents), the number of minutes spent and frequency of communication (weak relationship) were found to be related to WLC.

The different results for women are intriguing, though we are not able to offer a very definitive explanation. One plausible explanation is that women typically carry a higher burden of household responsibilities and are, therefore, more comfortable with and attuned to interruptions and multitasking. The frequency and volume of communication can potentially involve more interruptions, and the ability to attend to multiple threads of communication seamlessly therefore might not cause high levels of WLC. Given their dual domain responsibilities, it is possible that they are pressed for time and account for mobile use differently, focusing on clock time. The reason for the difference among the UK-US and Indian respondents is also not obvious, but might be attributed to smartphone adoption not being the norm among Indian IT professionals when the data was collected (between the years 2009 and 2012). More research is needed to uncover the underlying reasons for these patterns.

We now turn our attention to an in-depth qualitative study of IT professionals and consultants who were using mobile technology, and elaborate on their experiences. We also discuss some strategies that participants indicated they were using or proposed to use to manage the WLC of these individuals when applicable.

Findings from the Qualitative Study

Qualitative inquiry can often be valuable in gaining more in-depth insight into the phenomenon of interest, and to unearth *the how* and *the why* of the phenomenon. Our interviews suggest that the effects which increase the level of WLC may be categorized into four areas.

1. *Constantly Raising Expectations of Availability*

First and foremost, the use of mobile technologies provided by and paid for by the employer revises the psychological contract between employer and employee by constantly raising expectations of availability and the ability of the employee to respond. For example, one of our interviewees, a Senior Consultant in a leading consulting organization, stated:

> … [because clients/project-team members] know that you have a company-issued smartphone, they feel no shame in contacting you any time of the day or night. I receive calls, emails at 8, 9, 10 o'clock at night. Unfortunately, [because of the calls] you have to get up, and get out the laptop to produce some work at a ridiculous time …

2. *Blurring Boundaries of Work and Personal Time*

Second, while mobile technologies undoubtedly facilitate flexibility and free people from restricted hours and physical locations, they also blur boundaries of work and personal time (Chen & Karahanna, 2014). Many of our interviewees made this point. For example, a Director of a consulting organization said:

> … there is a constant expectation that I am connected … any time between 7 am and 10 pm … if you respond to one email at 8 pm then you are probably expected to respond to another at 8:30.

A Senior Consultant said:

> I think… mobile technology…basically chains you to your job. You don't have separation anymore.

Likewise, a Manager of a global software company noted:

> … there are new apps—more like instant messaging— [that] we now have on our phone, so people don't even know if I'm on my computer or my phone. And you are always online … so I am online at midnight, my phone vibrates. It is like a text message, except it uses the same application we

use at work. Email is bad enough, but now you can just instant message people, and they don't know what device they are instant messaging [to].

3. *Coordinating Among Coworkers Becomes More Complicated*

Because of the flexibility enabled by mobile technologies, coordination among coworkers becomes much more complicated, which in turn leads to further stretching of work–life boundaries. One of our respondents, a former CIO of a healthcare organization, observed:

> With mobile technology, you now have the flexibility of managing things 24x7, but there is no definition about what that availability should be. I [may] happen to be working, for example, at 8 pm because I went to a child's soccer game from 6 to 7:30. But since you have a mobile device, you [are expected to] be available, but you may be doing other things. So, it creates some discords because we don't sync up any more.

4. *Feeding Knowledge-Workers' Personal Compulsions*

Many knowledge workers feel the compulsion to be constantly on top of new developments pertaining to their responsibilities. The use of mobile technologies, and the convenience of being always connected, rather than "booting up" the computer or laptop, feeds this compulsion. The downside is that always being connected causes them to experience work-related stress around the clock. It can also strengthen the tendency for knowledge workers to find escape in their work. Both of these effects can, in time, cost employees their personal health and well-being, as the interviewee quotations below illustrate. A former CIO of a healthcare organization recalled rather ruefully how he sometimes fails to avoid sleeplessness at night:

> I make the mistake that I think many people [make] of checking work email at 11 pm when I am about to get ready for bed, and [find] something jarring in [an] email. I kick myself: 'why did I do that?'

An IT documentation specialist at a consulting organization also discussed how sleep patterns can be disturbed:

> … sometimes you're just waiting for [an] important email … and you want to check and make sure everything's okay. But the bad thing is, when your phone beeps at 3 am … you want to check it out. You have to break out of that [habit]… otherwise you are a slave to [the technology].

A Senior IT consultant of a consulting organization seemed all but resigned to losing his WLB:

> If you talk about work-life balance, I don't actually have any. I think a smartphone… is actually decreasing work-life balance.

Similar regret was expressed by a consulting partner who mentioned, with a hint of sadness, that she had given up all her friends and hobbies.

In summary, mobile technologies seem to contribute to the work–life conflict of knowledge workers in a variety of ways, increasing their stress levels as well as negatively influencing their family and social lives (e.g., Chen & Karahanna, 2014). In time, for many individuals and their organizations, these impacts can result in serious consequences.

Three Conceptions That Individuals Hold About the Relationship Between Their Work and Life Domains

An important insight from this study is that a very relevant difference between individuals was how they viewed work and life and the relationship between them. This is consistent with findings from previous research. For example, Dumas and Sanchez-Burks (2015, p. 805) note that individuals perceive their work–life relationship varying on a continuum they refer to as the "Integration-Segmentation Continuum." We introduce three perspectives, or worldviews, as *compartmentalized*, *overlapping*, and *encompassing*, which we elaborate on in this chapter (see Fig. 5.1). Past research on individual differences has focused on roles, gender, marital status, and so on, and the impact of such variables is, at best, mixed across different studies in different contexts. Our interviews appeared to suggest that these conceptions promise to be more useful than using traditional demographic attributes to managing WLC challenges.

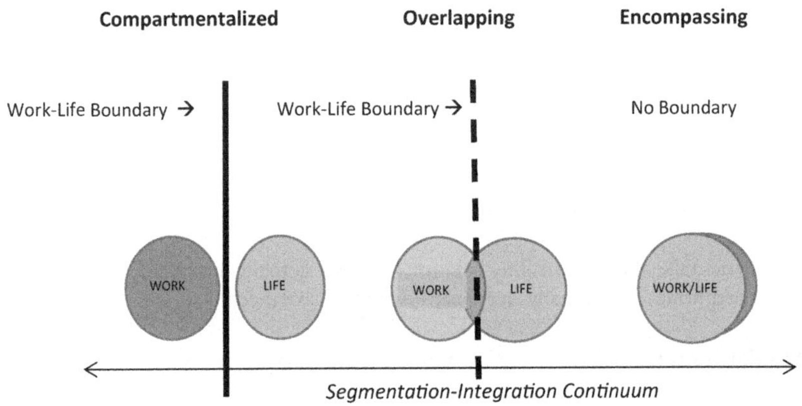

Fig. 5.1 Three perspectives on the relationship between personal life and work

The Compartmentalized Perspective

This worldview holds that work and life domains should be kept separate and protected from incursions from the other domain at any cost. Individuals subscribing to this perspective tend to prefer strict spatial and temporal boundaries between work and life domains. However, the need for "speed of response/reaction" now dominates much of knowledge-workers' daily working life. This need means that knowledge workers who hold the compartmentalized perspective will strive harder—and probably unsuccessfully—to keep the work and personal life domains separate. One of our interviewees put it like this:

> I want a 9 to 5 job. I don't care if I don't get promoted in five years … I'll do whatever you give me between 9 and 5. Don't give me an assignment outside of that.

Others indicated their yearning for a psychological separation between work and personal life:

> To me it's being able to let go at the end of the day and 100% invest my concentration, my time, my happiness into my family or leisure activity, or hobby or flat [apartment] where I'm not thinking about work to any degree.

Knowledge workers who hold the compartmentalized perspective tend to see personal life as primary and work as secondary. Most recognize the utility of work, which they view as the means to live a good life because, in return for their work, they have the means to support their personal aspirations, a certain lifestyle, and their hobbies. One of our interviewees (a senior consultant at a major US consulting company) told us that his passion is to be a photographer (rather than a consultant). He chose consulting as a profession primarily for the money it provides to support photography. For him, the compensation from work enabled him to lead a more satisfying life, and he expected to have a limited interference of life by demands of work. Several of our interviewees even felt that their work was a burden, and was preventing them from achieving what they truly desired as human beings. For example, they mentioned that work demands had caused them and their colleagues to give up their hobbies and had harmed their health. In one case, work demands had resulted in divorce and loss of meaning in life. Other factors that determine a knowledge worker's perspective on the work–life relationship include an individual's stage of life, career ambition, and job characteristics. Some revealed that individuals whose careers had plateaued were more likely to regard work as a separate part of life. And individuals with significant family responsibilities (e.g., especially women with young children) were more likely to hold the compartmentalized perspective.

Mobile Technology Use Patterns in Those Holding a Compartmentalized Perspective

Because people who hold the compartmentalized perspective see a clear boundary between work and personal life, they view mobile technologies as just another tool to get their work done efficiently, but do not voluntarily use mobile devices for work purposes after hours. They tend to manually disable certain functions of mobile devices (e.g., turning off emails) after hours or during weekends so that they can "switch off" from work, focus on their personal life, and have "peace of mind." Some in this category even perceive mobile technologies as a tool that others can use to track them. Indeed, a consultant in a well-known consulting company said that she had chosen not to get a work phone because she did not want colleagues to contact her, and she did not even want to be aware of work-related issues after hours:

> I was one of the last people … to get a smartphone, because I didn't want 24x7 email. When I left work, that was that. I didn't check anything, I didn't look at anything.

The Overlapping Perspective

This worldview acknowledges that work and life domains cannot be kept isolated because the nature of certain jobs necessitates working from home and beyond formal office hours (e.g., attending to work issues during family time and in the family place), just as it might be necessary to leave work to attend a meeting with the teachers of a child in school (i.e., attending to family issues) during work time. This perspective acknowledges the need for flexibility and stretching of the boundaries between work and life domains, and occasional incursions of work demands into personal life domains. As such, this perspective is more consistent with the current working environment of knowledge workers. Individuals who hold this perspective assume that, although the two domains may have "physical and temporal boundaries," there are "emotional and behavioral" overlaps between the two, and this overlap leads to each domain affecting the other in positive or negative ways (Clark, 2000). Although individuals who hold the overlapping perspective may accept this overlap, they tend to face high degrees of conflict as they attempt to balance the two domains, especially as they need to accommodate more and more incursions of work into their lives. With knowledge work, spillover between work and life domains is unavoidable and sometimes even desirable. Many knowledge workers who hold the overlapping perspective seem to view work as a necessary aspect of a fulfilling life. However, they are keen to limit the importance of work to avoid being totally swamped by it or to prevent it from hijacking their life goals. A consultant stated:

> Work is important to me, and I get satisfaction from work, but I also put lots of emphasis on my life outside of work too. So, I don't feel like I need to work 24x7. There are times when I can just put it away and that's it.

People holding the overlapping perspective don't mind some spillover of work into personal life. However, they usually have a "zone of tolerance"—i.e., the number (or extent) of work-related incursions they would readily allow into their personal life domains beyond normal work hours. The tolerance level is fairly elastic for most individuals, but it does depend on factors such as the nature and urgency of the work concerned, the individual's motivation (e.g., financial or career aspirations), and stage of life. It also depends on whether the individual is dealing with additional family-related responsibilities at the time, and whether the line manager has consultatively attempted to harmonize the additional work demands with the personal circumstances. About 60% of our interviewees fell into the overlapping perspective category because of the nature of their job requirements as well as the high level of connectivity enabled by mobile and other technologies. With increased globalization and offshoring, it is not uncommon for knowledge workers such as IT professionals to have to collaborate with individuals across different time zones, making it much more difficult to have a clear boundary between work and personal life. Moreover, knowledge workers in important roles or with career growth aspirations are often expected not to openly prioritize personal time over work time. In some companies, for example, it would become an issue if employees routinely chose not to respond to emails after hours.

Mobile Technology Use Patterns of Those Holding an Overlapping Perspective

Individuals holding the overlapping perspective appear to have mixed feelings about the use of mobile technologies. On the one hand, they might have an urge to constantly check their emails so they can attend to urgent issues or, at the least, maintain awareness of developments. On the other hand, they feel the need to limit their use of mobile technologies beyond the workday. Notably, some knowledge workers are happy to allow spillovers as long as they are compensated. In the words of a security administrator of a higher education organization:

> [Being contacted by phone over the weekends doesn't happen] a lot. If [it did], it would irritate me ... It doesn't feel like an invasion to me, because I feel I am compensated for that ... I feel I get compensated well enough for that, but I think the downside is I am never refreshed.

Others tolerate spillovers because they derive inherent satisfaction from work and from being valued members of their teams. For them, mobile technologies serve as a tool to keep them aware of what is going on and also help them to voluntarily attend to urgent work after hours, as mentioned by consultant:

> I like to see what is going on, I like to see my emails are coming through, but I also don't feel compelled that I have to respond to everything, that I have to really read everything in detail. I can kind of observe it … For the most part, I like to be aware, but when it is outside [business] hours, I don't necessarily feel compelled to have to respond to everything.

The Encompassing Perspective

Finally, this perspective holds that the individual's work and life are so intertwined together that they cannot be understood separately, in that the two domains almost entirely eclipse each other. Typically, the individuals are immersed in work to such an extent that they start to enact the view of *life is work*, and they might even seek *life within work.* Within the encompassing perspective of the work–life relationship, success in the work domain often equates to success in the personal life domain. Individuals who hold this perspective do not see boundaries that separate work and personal life, and often embrace the positives that work brings to their nonwork life (and vice versa). Such individuals tend to unequivocally prioritize work over personal and family commitments, filling their personal life with their hectic, though often self-defined, work schedules. One of our interviewees, a former CIO of a healthcare firm, provided an interesting historical justification for the integration of work and personal life:

> The concept of strict separation of work and personal life is really [a modern] phenomenon. If you look back [in history] people's work and home life were fully integrated. If you lived in the United States, [every] small town and village [had its own] blacksmith, doctor [and other] professions … they [worked] when other people in the town needed them. It's only [since] the industrial revolution and formation of offices [that] people left their home environment [to go to work]. So, I think what we are seeing now is the potential of swinging back with technology-mediated work [to a] fully integrated. [work/personal life environment]

The encompassing perspective is often held by individuals who love their work intrinsically relative to other personal leisure options or are driven to succeed and seek to progress very rapidly in the organization. Many of these individuals don't particularly feel the need to compartmentalize their work and personal life or to choose personal time over work time. For them, nothing is more important than work. In a sense, they could be classified as individuals who live to work. Indeed, some see living to work as the most productive way to spend their time at their particular phase of life. For example, in the words of a senior program manager of a software company:

> I am really focused on my career. I feel like I am doing really good, so I am trying to hit when the iron is hot, so that's where I am right now … work as life. I am trying to take advantages of the opportunities in front of me.

Another quote, from an individual who had headed a major Korean IT Consulting firm, illustrates the implications of holding this perspective:

> To me, life means life within the company … while working … you don't have any life that is traditionally defined. But we have life while working … [but a] compromised one… If we want to succeed within the company, we find kind of a compromised way to enjoy life while working … life seems to be realized or vitalized within the workplace without … family.

In many of the firms our interviewees worked for, a large proportion of jobs simply require employees to work long hours and to be available 24 × 7 to engage with work-related issues. In such situations, the characteristics and responsibilities of their jobs force people to adopt the "live to work" mode. Individuals who are just starting their careers in highly competitive companies are more likely to hold the encompassing perspective, at least until they feel they are established and perceive that they are adding value to the company. Likewise, as seen above, individuals who see growth opportunities if they excel in a particular phase of their career tend to let work encompass their personal lives.

Mobile Technology Use Patterns in Those Holding the Encompassing Perspective

People holding the encompassing perspective of the work–life relationship have a predominantly positive view of mobile technologies because these technologies support their work styles by providing 24 × 7 connectivity. The use of mobile technologies enables them to integrate work into their lives because they can work anywhere (and whenever) they want. In the words of a product manager of a software development company:

> … it is simpler and easier to get connected, be connected and stay connected for those of us who have tendencies to live that way anyway … just like a laptop frees you from a desktop computer, enables you to move around, a smartphone or iPad frees you from the laptop … So, for example, I can go to my son's gym class and yet I can actually do a little bit work on my iPad while he's there.

Another interviewee, a senior manager of a software development company, told us:

> We never really ever have to disconnect. So, if I am at the gym, I will check my phone. Then if I have an email, I will stop running and respond … I usually just check my email whenever… no cut-off line at night.

In many of these cases, we noticed that it is not particular job demands, but incongruence between the worldview and the job demands, which lead to a perception of high WLC and other negative effects. It then follows that organizational policies such as: "we are moving the company's employees toward work-life integration," or "we encourage employees to shut off their office mobile phones after work-hours," are not necessarily helpful, and can be counter-productive, depending on the worldview and the context of the individual. Interestingly, our interviews suggest that a preference for the compartmentalized perspective often signifies to others a lack of motivation and commitment.

Strategies for Managing WLC

Having looked at the different work–life perspectives and the mobile device use patterns of individuals with different perspectives, let us now discuss some of the strategies that organizations or managers might use to manage WLC. The key strategies we identified were: the separation strategy, the compensation strategy, the facilitation strategy, the integration strategy, and finally, the protection strategy (see Table 5.1).

The Separation Strategy

This strategy enables individuals to protect their personal time and space from incursion by work demands. This could include institutional mandates of not working beyond a certain number of hours each day,

Table 5.1 Organizational strategies for addressing WLC concerns

Strategies	*Summary*
Separation	Enabling individuals to protect their personal time and space from incursion by work demands
Compensation	Setting up incentives that are provided to employees as an exchange for allowing a specific amount of work to spill over to their personal life domain
Facilitation	Optimizing, through consultation and participation, (a) the demands of the job, which employees need to successfully accomplish, (b) their personal life requirements, and (c) the employee's assumptions regarding work and life boundaries desired
Integration	Erasing much of the boundary between work and life domains of employees and enabling them to seamlessly move between work and personal life domains at all times
Protection	Isolating and sheltering employees from colleagues/managers/subordinates who see significant overlaps or integration of work and life as an imperative for accomplishing work efficiently and effectively, and who may thus choose to impose this way of life on colleagues, subordinates, and sometimes, even superiors

not taking any phone calls, or even checking or responding to emails outside office hours. A manager in Finland offered an example, where, some employees would report any attempt to make an incursion into pre-agreed nonwork time, and Human Resources (HR) would then get involved:

> ..there are two profiles of people... [one profile is..] ... if I was setting up a meeting with a person that is outside the box we just drew at 7 pm [i.e., scheduled end of work time], they will totally reject me. They will even contact HR and say this guy is crazy. What [do] they expect me to do, work [after] 7 pm in the evening, no way, I am not going to do that... The HR will contact you if you.. don't play according to the rules...

A technical architect employed in a leading multinational in India provided another example of separation:

> When I was saying [to the company] that I can't take calls during these [certain times], at least till my son starts reacting not so violently to it, they [managers] were fine with it. Again, that is an individual requirement.

> Some people have different requirements and I think [company name] ...tries to accommodate most of them.

In terms of mobile technologies, many companies, for example, provide smart work-phones that must be switched off or left at work at the end of the workday and restarted when work hours begin again.

The Compensation Strategy

Another straightforward strategy that has been adopted by many companies is that of compensating employees for the additional time that they might spend working. In pursuing this strategy, the company attempts to compensate employees for the sacrifices they make to get the work done. This strategy is applied to all employees regardless of their role, gender, stage in life, or circumstances. Typically, compensation is in the form of monetary rewards or time off. However, one view of this strategy is that it does not really address WLC but merely provides incentives for employees to overlook the problem. One of our interviewees referred to this strategy as applying a "band-aid."

Our interviews also indicated that the compensation strategy is effective only for certain types of individuals—those who are in it for the money. Those who are financially "comfortable," or not overly motivated by extrinsic means, would not be helped by this strategy. Managers should, therefore, not assume that spillovers will be tolerated by such employees on a continuous basis just because they are being compensated. One of our interviewees, a former CIO, reflected on the indiscriminate use of the compensation strategy to stretch employees' work time (through, for example, expectations about employees' mobile connectivity):

> No, I don't think that [compensation] works ... it is a leadership cop-out ... It is just an easy thing to do. I think that weak leadership will try that sort of thing ... I think the most effective way from the business perspective is to be very clear about what the objectives are, and define what those are and give people the flexibility to meet those objectives.

Even though some managers considered the compensation strategy to be ineffective, we believe it is relevant for knowledge workers who view work and life as compartmentalized but can be motivated by financial or other incentives to tolerate some degree of spillovers for very short periods. This strategy is also relevant to knowledge workers who view work as overlapping with life, in that it provides them with tangible reassurance that the company appreciates their contributions, which might involve working beyond standard working hours.

Facilitation Strategy

The above quote from a former CIO in the "compensation strategy" section suggests that facilitation may be a better strategy than compensation for managing spillovers of work into employees' personal lives. The facilitation strategy recognizes that it is not possible to achieve success in the current environment by maintaining rigid boundaries between work and personal life domains. Yet, unlike the compensation strategy, which tends to demand intense sacrifice in exchange for something attractive, the facilitation strategy takes a more empathetic and collaborative approach. Specifically, the goal is to limit the stress and WLC of employees by taking into consideration the personal situations and capabilities of the individual and harmonizing them with the demands of the project. For example, the project manager may designate different team members to be "on-call" and to monitor (late into the evening) the project status in offshore locations on different days, based on their family-related commitments (e.g., child's soccer game) on given days. Likewise, the manager may grant a long-overdue two-week vacation to an employee with the understanding that he or she would check emails each morning and be available to attend the Monday morning coordination meeting remotely. One of our interviewees, a former CIO of a healthcare organization, explained:

> … We do this for groups across many different types of dimensions, not just mobile devices and work-life balance … I always work with teams to go through a very intentionally facilitated process to define how we want to work together as a team

From our interviews, we conclude that managers should consider devising mechanisms to allow employees to dynamically provide input on their preferences and changing circumstances. For the facilitation strategy to be effective, employees need to let their stakeholders, such as their managers, colleagues, and clients, know how much overlap between work and personal life domains they are prepared to tolerate in terms of mobile connectivity and responsiveness, and specify their preference for the nature of temporal or spatial boundary incursions that they could handle. Note that the facilitation strategy requires significant preparation on the part of management, in terms of understanding different employees' preferences and constraints, and then matching the project requirements with employee preferences. Only then can harmony be achieved between work and life for the employees while also meeting the organization's role. We believe that decision support systems with artificial intelligence (AI) components can be particularly useful in supporting the facilitation approach.

Our research shows this strategy is usually implemented by mid-level managers (e.g., project managers or team leaders) in the form of informal procedures, norms, and rules. Given the informal nature of policy implementation in this area, the key to an effective facilitation strategy is for managers to create an environment where colleagues are trusting of each other and respectful of each other's work–life boundaries. One of our interviewees, a director of a consulting firm, highlighted this issue:

> ... if you send an email [to your staff] and you are a very high [level] partner ... and they see it at 10 pm at night, they are going to think they need to respond. And it could be the only reason it went out is because you just landed somewhere. But you never said that ... So, having a line in the email that says, 'No need to respond to this tonight' [would be] really [helpful]. [Senior people should] remember that not everybody is [necessarily] connected ... as [they] are... I think it would be [good] to have a policy [on this]... Formalization of some of the informal policies, without making the process too inflexible and bureaucratic, can sometimes be useful.

We note that the above ideas are consistent with the three principles for facilitation proposed by Friedman et al. (1998): First, managers need to be clear in informing employees about the organization's work-related needs and priorities and simultaneously encourage employees to articulate their own personal nonwork needs and priorities. Second, managers need to "recognize and support their employees as whole people," ensuring that both work and nonwork needs are being accommodated and actually celebrated. Third, they need to "continually experiment" with the way they allocate and accomplish tasks, such that iteratively, work, and nonwork needs are met optimally.

Being inherently flexible and consultative in nature, the facilitation strategy can have some degree of relevance even for knowledge workers who view work as compartmentalized from life, as well as for those who view work as overlapping with life.

Integration Strategy

Many forward-looking companies are openly acknowledging that achieving a work–life balance may not be a viable goal, and are thus promoting the idea of integration. For example, a manager of a global IT company in India noted:

> We're moving away from that term [WLB]... We now talk about work-life integration. Nobody talks about work-life balance anymore.

The integration strategy implies that work and personal life domains are so interconnected that they become inseparable, and the boundaries between them become meaningless. This strategy focuses on creating an inviting environment where employees experience (much of) their personal life in the workplace, thereby allowing those who are sufficiently motivated or committed to immerse themselves in work not to feel they are missing out on life outside their organization. One of our respondents from a leading Aerospace company described the integration strategy that one of her friends in an innovative IT company really liked:

> They get a lot of perks to be able to work there, they have ... more flexibility. One [perk] I would be really excited about is you can bring your dog to work and have periodic breaks during the day to walk [the dog]. [It means you have some].. work-life balance during work.

However, our interviewees made it clear that the *integration strategy is not for everyone*; only those who, in our opinion, hold the encompassing perspective can function and thrive in an environment that promotes integration. The integration strategy is, therefore, appropriate only for individuals for whom the encompassing perception of the work–life relationship is predominant.

Protection Strategy

Oftentimes, there is a need to shield individuals (especially those holding a compartmentalization perspective, and sometimes even those holding an overlapping perspective) from the influence and pressures of those holding the encompassing perspective, with a presumed 24 × 7 connectivity and responsiveness, and indubitably higher priority of work over personal life demands. For example, one of our interviewees, the owner of a small web development firm, told us:

> I think there is a major difference between [people who] value work-life balance [differently]. I think that [difference] can cause some friction. [On the other hand], if two people have the same views [on work-life balance], that may cause some synergies.

He also mentioned that he "felt guilty" for trying to balance his work and life whenever he worked with team members and managers who "live to work." Another interviewee, a Project Manager in consulting, highlighted the challenges he had faced when working with colleagues who hold different perspectives on the relationship between work and life:

> The people who will always put life ahead of work [i.e., who approach their work as] 'I will get to it when I get to it' [tend to] put additional stress on the rest of the team … trying to achieve a deadline.

Along the same lines, a senior manager of a global software company, who considered himself as holding the encompassing perspective, talked about his frustrations of working with team members who sought to separate their work and personal life domains or prioritized personal time over work. He said their attitudes "drove me crazy." However, he also sensed he was paying the price for his attitude and perceived that he "turned people off" and was starting to "step on people's toes." We believe that many employees who were being "turned off" or "whose toes were being stepped on" would consider leaving the company. We feel that even those holding the encompassing perspective should have some degree of protection from themselves, because long periods of overlap between work and life could start taking a toll on the personal and health front.

A well-formulated protection strategy is needed in such cases. Protection has two aspects: first, the organization must attempt to ensure that the expectation of sustained (even if voluntary) connectivity does not

Table 5.2 Matching work–life perspectives with strategies

Perspective on the relationship between work and life	*Separation*	*Compensation*	*Facilitation*	*Integration*	*Protection*
Compartmentalized (*work as segmented from life*)	**H**	M	M	L	**H**
Overlapping (*work as part of life*)	L	**H**	**H**	L	M
Encompassing (*work as inseparable from life*)	L	M	M	**H**	M

H = High Relevance
M = Medium or possible relevance
L = Low or unlikely relevance

affect the health and personal well-being of valuable individuals, including those who hold the encompassing perspective. This can be done through corporate wellness programs tailor-made for each individual. Second, the organization must enact policies that guard subordinates and colleagues, who do not relate to the integration of work and life domains, from individuals who would potentially want to impose their encompassing perspective on them. Going even further, we might say that the protection strategy is relevant for all knowledge workers. Organizations need to protect those knowledge workers who view their work as encompassing life from burning out while also protecting other knowledge workers who don't hold this encompassing perspective from being forced to work this way by colleagues and supervisors. In Table 5.2, we have indicated the level of relevance for each of the five strategies to individuals with different perspectives of the work–life relationship.

Some Broad Guidelines for Managing a Mobile Workforce

Before proceeding with the guidelines, let us bring Border Theory, introduced in Chapter 1, into the discussion. The study is concerned primarily with challenges that border crossers (discussed in Chapter 3) face. Mobile technology makes the borders between work and life extremely permeable. Yet, different border crossers appear to experience WLC differently. Why is this so? We believe it is because of the assumptions they hold about the nature of border desirable between work and life. When their border crossing experiences in their professional (or personal) situations do not quite match their assumptions, they experience high WLC. This implies that WLC should be assessed based on what is subjectively experienced, and not necessarily based on absolute values of certain variables such as the level of temporal flexibility of the individuals' schedule. Furthermore, border keepers need to understand that management of WLC of border crossers is deeply contextual, based on different categories of variables outlined by Border Theory, but most importantly, the border-crossers' assumptions regarding the ideal nature of the work–life border.

In other words, we believe that *there can be no universal solution to WLC challenges* faced by the mobile workforce because different people hold different perspectives on work–life relationships, and consequently, they have very different preferences on how to handle conflicts between work and personal life domains. However, this does not mean that organizations should ignore the problem. Rather, there is a need for a range of solutions that are sensitive to the needs of specific situations and preferences of knowledge workers. Though it is not necessary to put in place a tailor-made plan for each individual (indeed, this would be impractical), organizations do need policies that are sensitive to the range of reactions to WLC issues arising from the use of mobile technologies. The policies should also take into account how individuals' attitudes to WLC might vary by factors such as organizational role, and stage of life. Based on our interviews with a broad range of IT professionals (who we believe are representative of knowledge workers in general), we provide six guidelines for managing a mobile workforce in a way that minimizes work–life conflicts.

Guideline 1: Acknowledge That Different Individuals Perceive the Relationship Between Their Work and Life Very Differently

It is amply clear that all individuals do not experience WLC for the same reasons, as suggested by the fact that different individuals hold different perspectives of the work–life relationship (see Fig. 5.1). Work can be viewed as being separate from life, overlapping with life, or even as encompassing life. Moreover, individuals might shift with respect to the perspective they hold during their professional lifetime—depending on their stage in life or as their personal circumstances and aspirations change over time.

Guideline 2: Universal Strategies for the Use of Mobile Technologies *Are Unlikely to Be Effective*

It is helpful for managers to be cognizant of how their employees view work in the context of their lives. In other words, when feasible, managers need to place each employee (at a given point of time) on the continuum shown in Fig. 5.1. Indeed, our findings may provide an explanation of why practitioners and academics alike report that universal organizational policies fail to tackle WLC issues in organizations. Given the vast differences in how different individuals perceive the relationship between work and life, broad-brush strategies aimed at all the employees for managing the use of mobile technologies are unlikely to be effective. Knowledge workers (apart from the relatively few who view their work and personal life domains as completely separate) appear to have a zone of tolerance with respect to their WLC. For example, individuals positioned near the middle point of the continuum cannot be infinitely pushed with respect to their work. While such individuals may indeed allow, or even welcome, a certain level of overlap between their work and personal life domains to get the job done, there is an upper limit to how much they can tolerate. Sustained periods of higher-than-normal spillover of work into personal life, even when well-compensated, may result in breakdowns in an employee's personal relationships or mental/physical health, and, consequently, lead to increased staff turnover and lower productivity over time.

Guideline 3: Strategies to Meet the Organization's Overall Mobility Goals Should Cause Minimal WLC for Individual Employees

Once organizations recognize the different perspectives on work–life relationship held by their employees, they can focus on choosing the appropriate strategy for managing their mobile technology usage: separation, compensation, negotiating, integration, or protection. For example, employees who see work as encompassing life should be managed using tactics of integration—in terms of technology infrastructure, policies, and nature of responsibilities assigned—that are geared toward allowing them to move seamlessly across work and personal life domains. Intelligent technologies may be designed to support boundary management customization for individuals with different assumptions and circumstances.

Guideline 4: Mobile Technologies Should Be Implemented Consistent with Employees' Perspectives Regarding the Relationship Between Work and Life

Organizations need to encourage innovative design and use of mobile technologies while being sensitive to the differences in employees' perspectives of the work–life relationship. For example, individuals who view work and personal life as compartmentalized could benefit from having two mobile devices, one paid for by the company, which they switch off after work hours, and another self-funded device they would use at other times (if they so desired). Given that carrying two phones is inconvenient, organizations could consider deploying devices that can use or switch between two SIM cards, one for business purposes (with charges paid for by the employer) and the other for personal use (charges paid by the individual). For individuals who hold the overlapping perspective, and thus feel the need to constrain the compulsion to be connected all the time, organizations can encourage the use of apps with the default capability to switch off connections to corporate email and data server at predetermined times. On days the individual is required to maintain mobile connectivity beyond work time, the app would manage the individual's connections, the nature of connections (i.e., level of incursions, and the media of connection such as voice calls, email, and text) according to his or her personal life constraints, and keep track of times (beyond regular hours) and the specific official activities in which the individual may have participated. Such an app could generate periodic reports, which could serve as the basis for recognition or additional compensation. Individuals who hold the encompassing perspective would welcome mobile devices that could seamlessly integrate work into their personal lives. Organizations should ensure that these individuals are able to access and manipulate corporate data and applications from their mobile devices anywhere and anytime, thereby increasing their productivity. Finally, the policies many organizations have prohibiting the use of company mobile devices for personal activities are obviously inconsistent with the needs of those who hold the encompassing perspective. Such policies should be reconsidered.

Guideline 5: Proposed Strategies and Suggestions Should Be Applied with Caution

There was no specific evidence in our study to suggest that cultures necessarily have a notable impact on individuals' perceptions of the work–life relationship or their views on mobile technology usage. However, different countries do have their own labor laws, and different companies have different work cultures and social contracts between employees and employers that shape the expectations of employees regarding WLC. These differences can have potential implications for how WLC-related issues should be handled. This requires managers, especially of companies that operate globally, to apply the strategies and suggestions we propose in this article with caution, taking account of the particular legal, regulatory, and social environments of the relevant national contexts.

Concluding Comments

Our survey data suggest that, overall, for IT professionals working in a distributed context, higher the extent of communication using a mobile device, and higher the proportion of an individual's tasks potentially involving the use of mobile devices, higher the resulting level of WLC. Furthermore, higher WLC is associated with higher levels of synchronous communication engaged in, as part of work.

The interviews with IT professionals using mobile technologies also suggest that to minimize conflict between their work and life, an understanding of the different perspectives (compartmentalized, overlapping, and encompassing) they hold on the relationship between work and personal life, may be necessary. The management strategies we have identified (separation, compensation, facilitation, integration, and protection) for addressing the WLC issues arising from the use of mobile technologies need to be matched to the perspectives discussed, keeping the broad context in mind. Choosing the most appropriate strategy will allow individuals to achieve the optimal balance between their work and personal life, and ultimately reduce burnout, health problems, and turnover.

References

Adisa, T. A., Gbadamosi, G., & Osabutey, E. L. C. (2017). What happened to the border? The role of mobile information technology devices on employees' work-life balance. *Personnel Review, 46*(8), 1651–1671.

Chatterjee, S., Sarker, S., & Siponen, M. (2017). How do mobile ICTs enable organizational fluidity: Toward a theoretical framework. *Information & Management, 54,* 1–13.

Chen, A., & Karahanna, E. (2014). Boundaryless technology: Understanding the effects of technology-mediated interruptions across the boundaries between work and personal life. *AIS Transactions on Human-Computer Interaction, 6*(2), 16–36.

Clark, S. C. (2000). Work/family border theory: A new theory of work/family balance. *Human Relations, 53*(6), 747–770.

Dumas, T. L., & Sanchez-Burks, J. (2015). The professional, the personal, and the ideal worker: Pressures and objectives shaping the boundary between life domains. *Academy of Management Annals, 9*(1), 803–843.

Friedman, S. D., Christensen, P., & DeGroot, J. (1998). Work and life: The end of the zero-sum game. *Harvard Business Review,* 1–14. Reprint 98605.

Middleton, C. A. (2008). Do mobile technologies enable work-life balance? Dual perspectives on BlackBerry usage for supplemental work. In *Mobility and technology in the workplace* (pp. 209–221). Routledge.

Sarker, S., Xiao, X., Sarker, S., & Ahuja, M. (2012). Managing work-life balance of mobile technology-enabled IT workers: Perspectives and strategies. *MIS Quarterly Executive,* 143–157.

CHAPTER 6

Looking Back… and Looking Ahead

Broadly speaking, this book is about distributed work and human well-being, and it brings together a number of studies that we have undertaken over the last decade or so in this area. In this chapter, in addition to offering an integrative summary of our findings, we have taken the liberty to conclude the book with a section that we had not originally planned for. As we were in the process of wrapping up this book, we found ourselves in the midst of the COVID-19 pandemic. The pandemic appeared to highlight the relevance of many of the themes discussed in the earlier chapters of this book to people all around us, not just to distributed knowledge workers. Thus, we felt that it would be a good idea to analyze the current COVID-19 situation with a hypothetical scenario and to discuss some ideas, even if preliminary, for managing Work–Life Conflict (WLC) in a world where COVID and such pandemics might increasingly require knowledge workers and many others to work from home. We hope that some of our readers will relate to the scenario and find the analysis to be meaningful.

First, let us revisit some of the highlights from our earlier chapters. In Chapter 5, based on the study by Sarker et al. (2012) on the use of mobile technologies by professionals working in IT development and consulting, we discuss how different individuals appeared to have different conceptions regarding the relationship between work and life domains, that had a noticeable influence on the circumstances in which an individual felt a

S. Sarker et al., *Navigating Work and Life Boundaries*,
https://doi.org/10.1007/978-3-030-72759-8_6

lack of work–life balance. Further, the chapter highlighted the finding that individuals' own "conceptions" regarding the relationship between work and life affect how they perceive and respond to the different mitigation strategies that companies might employ. Leslie et al. (2019, p. 74) refer to these "conceptions" as "work-life ideologies." Specifically, the three conceptions we identified (compartmentalized, overlapping, and encompassing) have some similarity with the three ideologies proposed by Leslie et al. (2019): the "fixed-pie work-life ideology," the "segmentation work-life ideology," and the "work-priority ideology." We emphasize that these conceptions are not necessarily static and are shaped and reshaped over time by a variety of circumstances that likely result from interactions among different individual attributes, the phase of life, labor market, and so on. Furthermore, the work–life ideologies that different individuals hold may be more (or less) flexible (Leslie et al., 2019). We unearth a number of managerial strategies including separation, compensation, facilitation, integration, and protection, and show which strategy (or strategies) might be suited for individuals holding a particular work–life perspective or ideology.

Figure 6.1 shows some of the key elements associated with managing WLC. The box at the center represents the focal individual ("self") or the so-called "border crosser," who holds a certain work–life ideology at a given point of time. The circles represent various facets of work and life that share borders with the individual. In a sense, this forms the *constellation of relevant stakeholders* for the focal individual. Naturally, there may be partial overlaps between the constellations of different individuals. Family, friends, and community might represent elements in the "life" domain for an individual border crosser, while job situation, organization, and profession as well as subordinates and supervisors might represent elements in the "work" domain; technology could be part of either or both domains. Each of these elements of the constellation poses certain demands, and might offer resources to the focal individual seeking to create a balance (e.g., Wayne et al., 2019). For example, a family may need more physical co-presence of the individual (a "demand" by family), which can be enabled by the virtual communication and collaboration capability (a "resource" offered by the technology). This, in turn, might potentially allow the individual to stay home, as per demands of family, while also attending to work commitments (a demand of the work situation), and thereby avoid increased WLC. In summary, the figure

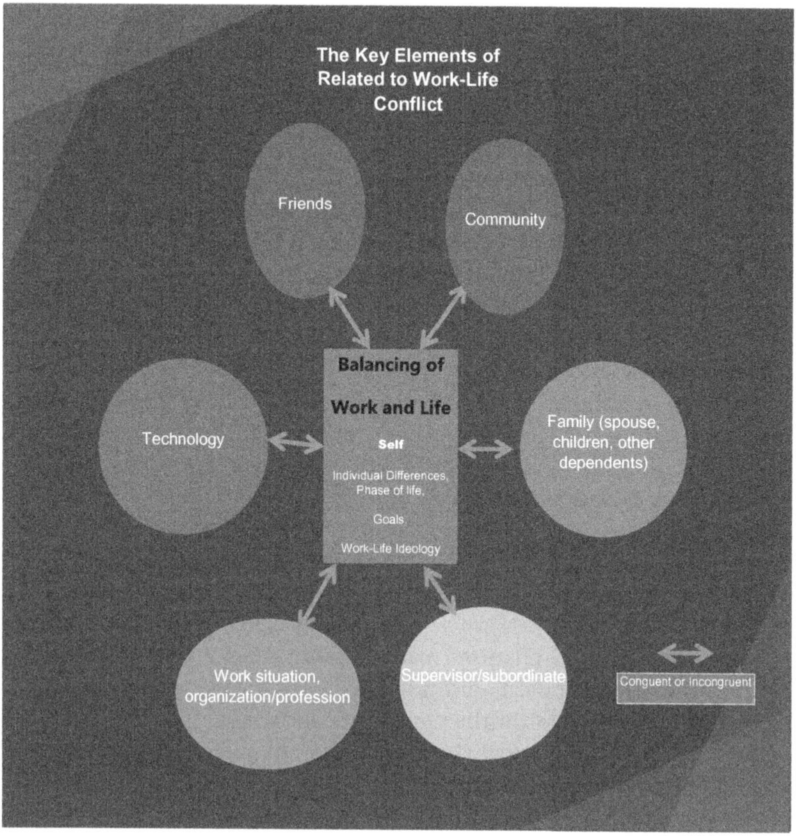

Fig. 6.1 Key elements influencing WLC of individuals

highlights our view that managing WLC entails overseeing a complex web of relationships and associated borders.

With respect to the *life domain*, different individuals may face different *family situations*. They could, for example, be single, have a working spouse or partner, have young children with special needs, and/or have family members who need care due to illness or disability. Each of these situations places different demands on the individual, and in the absence of adequate resources (e.g., time, or additional help) to deal with the demands, a higher level of WLC may be experienced. Likewise, friends and community (e.g., social clubs, church) may place demands on the focal individual but may also act as resources. For example, not being able to meet the demands of friends and community due to professional demands represents an incursion of work into the individual's life, potentially leading to increased WLC, as noted by one of our respondents, a consulting manager, in Chapter 5. In fact, she mentioned her deep sorrow for not being able to have a place for friends in her busy, professionally successful life. Further, there needs to be a high level of congruence between the work–life ideology and the demands the individual faces from the relevant constellation of elements associated with life as well as work. For instance, a person who believes in and identifies with the encompassing ideology is likely to have difficulty with a family, community, or set of friends that place demand on her time and attention by expecting her participation in activities, say, during weekends. Of course, the situation can change as the individual moves to a different phase of life, as suggested by a number of our interviewees. The individual's attributes and immediate circumstances could also influence the level of WLC. Specifically, in Chapter 3, we saw that the personality trait of neuroticism, caregiving of a dependent, national cultural context, and an individual's priority toward family influence her WLC. Interestingly, we found that gender, relation (marital) status, and the professional role (technical or non-technical) did not directly influence the level of WLC of the individual, at least in the context of our study.

With respect to the *work domain*, there are different aspects of the work situation that can tilt the scale of WLC unfavorably for the individual. For example, the IT profession is typically not considered to be compatible with the compartmentalized perspective, particularly when globally distributed work (where a clear "physical and temporal border" is absent") as part of offshoring is involved. Some methodologies (e.g., agile approaches such as Scrum) and work practices (e.g., flexible scheduling) representing "border permeability" and "border flexibility," respectively, may not be congruent with individuals with certain family situations, ideologies, and other characteristics, and their use can lead to insurmountable demand and consequently drained resources. On the other hand, some situations pertaining to jobs where there is an abundance of positions in the labor market may be more compatible with the compartmentalized conception. Similarly, incompatibility of work–life ideologies of the individual and his/her supervisors (the "border keepers") or even subordinates can lead to demands by the supervisor/subordinates that could, in the absence of compensating resources, or protection by the organization (see Chapter 5), lead to WLC concerns for the focal individual. In Chapter 2, we saw a number of empirical results related to the work domain. We found that the number of locations a distributed worker has to coordinate/collaborate with, the lack of work time overlaps between the worker and his/her remotely located collaborators, agile methodology use, task interdependence across locations ("dependency of the border crosser" with members in other locations), technological diversity across locations, requirements diversity, and requirements instability all affect WLC unfavorably (the last three factors are the "domain characteristics" of the work situation). Family friendly policies of companies helped reduce WLC, though the literature does warn about the potential "backlash" from such policies (Perrigino et al., 2018).

Finally, as mentioned earlier, technology can be burdensome and also serve as an invaluable resource for the individual. As seen in Chapter 5, mobile technologies can, for example, blur boundaries, and place demands in a way that is incongruent with the separation perspective held by individuals. Synchronous communication tools in an offshoring context can place serious demands on individuals holding all but the encompassing perspective, particularly for those whose family and community demand a lot of attention and time away from work.

A key takeaway we wish to emphasize is that managing WLC may be seen as a thorny optimization problem that involves managing time, strain, and behaviors (Greenhaus & Beutell, 1985, p. 76), given the different demands made by different stakeholders, the availability of different resources, and the constraints of relatively static individual ideologies and relevant individual differences. As discussed in Chapters 2 and 3, researchers have generally focused on the impact of individual demographics and circumstances (e.g., gender and involvement in dependent care) and of organizational initiatives (e.g., flextime and FFPs) on WLC, and these results have informed practice in the past. It is clear to us, based on our studies, that approaches such as "manipulating" variables within, say, the globally distributed work, without grasping the nuances of the context, seldom helps. For example, in Chapter 5, the implementation of family friendly policies, such as "picnics in the park with family" appeared to have little desirable effects on reducing WLC in an offshoring situation. Scholars have also proposed different approaches/processes, from separation to integration. Our work, particularly on mobile device use, suggests that the perspectives of individuals about work and life influence their WLC perceptions a great deal, and the attempt to managing WLC is necessarily contingent upon their perspectives. Yet, our reflections on the entire set of studies we conducted indicate to us that the work–life perspective is *just one of the many pieces of the WLC puzzle*. A dynamic and truly integrative approach of harmonizing the demands made and resources offered by different work and life domain elements is what is needed. Chapter 4 adds to the complexity of the phenomenon by highlighting broader organizational and strategic implications of WLC in distributed settings. It specifically shows that to have effective offshoring operations, WLC considerations for both onshore and offshore employees must be carefully understood and planned for—it is not sufficient to consider economic, legal, and other business environment concerns while overlooking human well-being concerns.

The COVID Crisis and the Death of Work–Life Balance?

The reader would perhaps agree that our discussion on WLC of those involved in distributed work, whether related to IT or other knowledge sectors, would be incomplete without at least introducing how the COVID-19 situation is making many aspects of our research relevant today. The crisis has made WLC a major issue for ***virtually everyone*** in societies with a certain level of IT availability, where people are not only getting work done but are ***actually living life*** in an IT-mediated distributed fashion.

The COVID-19 crisis and accompanying lockdowns (or near-lockdowns) in different parts of the world have affected knowledge workers in a variety of ways. Some feel that their productivity is up, others feel that their productivity is down (Liang, 2020). Some report sleeplessness and disorientation, yet others report more opportunity for self-care and exercise, and overall happiness (Nemko, 2020). Almost everyone appears to be experiencing some level of stress, with the constant mediation of ICTs in interacting with the outside world. Brod (1984, p. 16) defines this stress as "a modern disease of adaptation caused by an inability to cope with new computer technologies in a healthy manner." While some of this "technostress" may be positive (referred to as "eustress"), more often, it is negative stress (referred to as "distress") (Califf et al., 2019). The key questions that we wish to address, not with finality, but to start a conversation in light of what we know and what we may be experiencing, is: *What effect has the COVID-19 crisis and resulting lockdown had on knowledge-workers' WLC, and why?* More importantly, *what lessons do we have to offer, if any, for maintaining a manageable level of WLC in the current and post-COVID world*, at least in the short run.

To begin to address these issues in a somewhat concrete way, let us assume the following scenario set in North America. Admittedly, this is *just one scenario*, and we are aware that there are likely to be many different variations, based on the specific circumstances being faced by different individuals. Figure 6.2 represents a pre-COVID view of, in some

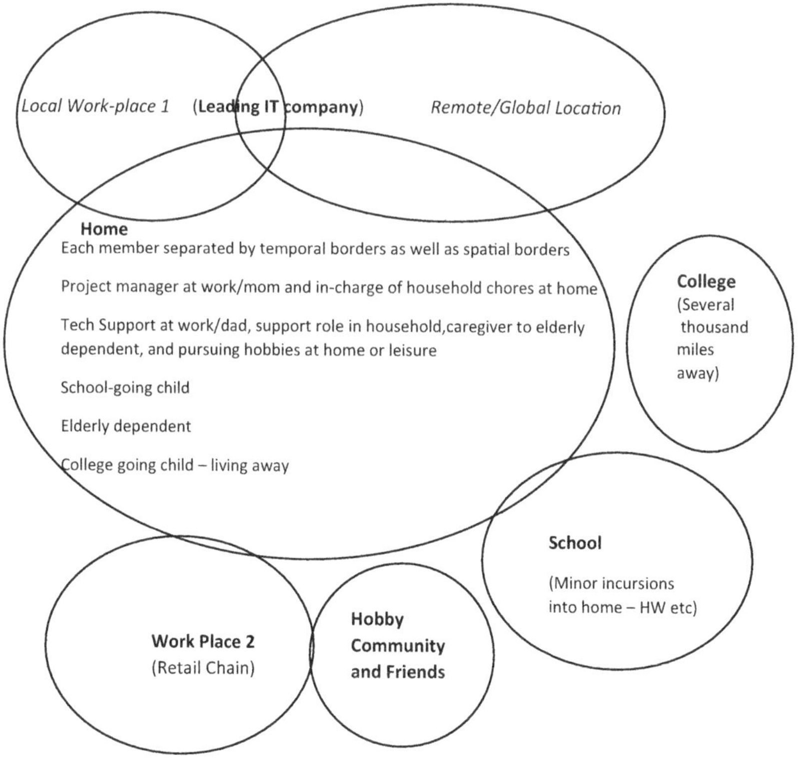

Fig. 6.2 Pre-COVID hypothetical scenario

sense, a traditional family of five, with two working parents, one school-going child and one college student (currently attending a university several thousand miles away), and an elderly grandparent, who stays home and needs some care, though she is able to stay by herself during the day-time when everyone is away. One parent (parent #1) works for a leading information technology company as a project manager, and she occasionally has to be in teleconferences during the evenings with colleagues from India and China. Though not a common occurrence, such sessions require her to sometimes get into the technical details of her projects and work collaboratively with colleagues in Asia using her laptop. When such situations present themselves, the work demands need to be given precedence over other demands. She prides herself as being the primary person in charge of family meals and care of children, including their homework. The other parent (parent #2) has a relatively steady end-user tech-support job at a national retail company, with work demands typically restricted to the time and place of work. This parent does have, and actively pursues other interests that are important to him, and he is "busy" in the evenings, typically two days a week, with friends who share the hobby. He is willing to take on a share of household chores and responsibilities related to the children, especially when needed. He is also the primary caretaker of the grandparent (his mother) who lives with them, and he spends about an hour each morning on chores related to her and interacting with her.

We assume the parent working as a project manager is committed to her career and has an "overlapping" work ideology, though with limits to how much she is willing to stretch her boundaries, while the other parent, in tech support, has a "compartmentalized" or "segmentation" mindset (see earlier chapters). Thus, prior to the onset of COVID-19, the work situations of both parents have had a degree of alignment with their work ideologies.

The COVID-19 crisis, with schools and workplaces moving online, introduces a number of changes to the work–life situation of this family, that can create serious WLC unless certain measures are taken by the family and/or the organizations they are part of.[1]

The first issue we notice is that *the entire family is confined to the same place* (e.g., Thomason & Williams, 2020) where work and personal life

[1] The discussion below focuses more on the complications and consequently the challenges to WLC posed. The enabling role of ICTs in keeping the society going, despite the lockdown, is unquestionable.

unfold for each member, who are, in addition, physically isolated from their social peers. While this could lead to better marriages, remove the need for long, daily commutes, and make it possible for individuals to spend more time with children (Liang, 2020), such confinement can, shockingly, have effects similar to being in prison. While we do not suggest that staying at home with family members is *the same as* being in prison, there are aspects of "prisonization" (especially those related to "house arrest") that may creep into the lives of family members. This could occur because of the seclusion from many preferred others, and ironically, more-than-usual association with some family members that the family members may have yearned for under normal circumstances. Depending on the traits of individuals involved and the characteristics of the family, prolonged "prisonization" may lead to "apathy" and "interpersonal distrust and suspicion" (concepts taken from Haney, 2001); some family members, especially children and dependents, may experience "emotional over-control" and may even engage in "social withdrawal and isolation" by "retreat[ing] deeply into themselves" (Haney, 2001). All of these are sources of *strain* that can contribute to the increasing WLC of individuals in the family.

The second issue is that *ICTs have become the sole and unavoidable window to the world.* ICTs have no doubt been a boon in this period of crisis, given that they have enabled online education, shopping, work, telehealth, and even social interactions among friends and family staying elsewhere. However, it is worth noting that much of the social interaction and collaboration at a distance is possible because of the *shared space* that these ICTs afford in lieu of a *shared place* that forms the context of much of meaningful human activity. In this regard, drawing on past works, Sarker and Sahay (2004, p. 4) note:

> Place and space reflect distinctive meanings and identifications of people to locations – physical or imagined... A place is like a 'home' laden with experience and meaning that helps to provide human beings with the sense of attachment, stability, and security. In contrast, a physical space of residence is more like a 'house' with little emotional and existential attachment (Eyles, 1989). While spaces represent arenas in which universalized and homogenized activities occur, places emphasize the need for situated and local action. Space and place thus conjure up various contrary and opposing images such as distance–proximity, universality–locality, standardization–particularity, and freedom–attachment.

In other words, despite arguments related to social presence (Short et al., 1976) and media expansion (Carlson & Zmud, 1999), the human connection and the gratification one achieves by relating to other humans, can only be partially achieved through ICTs (Sarker & Sahay, 2004), especially when such interaction is not intertwined with at least periodic co-presence, and occurring within a context that we associate with the given role we are enacting (Jiang, 2020). For example, we associate a bar with drinking in the company of friends. When this happens in a video chat from our offices at home, it does not provide the same gratifications associated with meeting friends in a bar. A prolonged lack of such gratification and absences of human contact can lead to strains in maintaining relationships and can also take away mental resources that help deal with psychological strains. Indeed, according to Lufkin (2020, para. 20), "Prolonged isolation could also potentially impact on morale and productivity." Moreover, "Zoom fatigue" and reports of extreme mental exhaustion as a result of videoconferencing are increasingly surfacing among those who use "video chats" constantly to participate in "work huddles, the one-on-one meetings and [at the end of the day]... the hangouts with friends and family" (Jiang, 2020, para. 1). There are several reasons why such fatigue is being experienced. Jiang reports, based on her interview with Petriglieri (para. 4)[2]:

> Being on a video call requires more focus than a face-to-face chat, says Petriglieri. Video chats mean we need to work harder to process non-verbal cues like facial expressions, the tone and pitch of the voice, and body language; paying more attention to these consumes a lot of energy. "Our minds are together when our bodies feel we're not. That dissonance, which causes people to have conflicting feelings, is exhausting. You cannot relax into the conversation naturally," he says.

Unlike watching television, when we get mental breaks, videoconferencing calls are "performative" as we are not only watching but also performing for the audience, since we are being watched back (Jiang, 2020). At a broader level, the strain may be associated with several dimensions of technostress. While there are a number of different aspects of technostress discussed in the literature (Ragu-Nathan et al., 2008), three

[2] Jiang's article is partly based on inputs from Gianpiero Petriglieri of INSEAD and Marissa Shuffler of Clemson University.

are particularly relevant for many of those adjusting to the COVID-induced lives. In words of Califf et al. (2019, pp. 812–813, italics added):

> *Techno-overload* occurs when individuals appraise events related to stressful situations that contribute to users having to work longer and faster than normal. *Techno-invasion* involves situations in which people are constantly connected to technology outside of the workplace context. *Techno-complexity* comprises situations in which the complexity of technology is associated with users feeling inadequate about their technology skills, resulting in users spending more time and effort to understand the technology (Tarafdar et al., 2011).

Obviously, those who are technologically savvy might not quite appreciate the technostress based on techno-complexity being experienced by those not so savvy. We would also like to note that while technostress cannot be equated to WLC, it is an important aspect of well-being, and it is known to affect WLC levels.

The third issue, related to the points made above, is that, *in many cases, boundaries or facades of boundaries related to work and life have been not just blurred, but erased*. The sharing of the same place *all the time* with family members with whom there have traditionally been temporal boundaries can add complications. For example, in the scenario discussed earlier, seeing that family members are at home may encourage the dependent (e.g., the grandparent) to seek attention and assistance at any time of the day. Children may also seek attention from their parents at any time of the day, irrespective of the job-related tasks the parents may be attending to at that time. As we have discussed in Chapter 3, parental responsibilities are increasingly being shared by both parents, but the women are often the ones whom children depend on, causing further strain-based and time-based conflict between the work and life domains (for women). A large proportion of families today also have a single parent (Thomason & Williams, 2020), which poses additional strain-based and time-based conflicts. Dizik (2020) observes that "Having kids can make you more productive – except when they're there all the time"; indeed, when men and women in full-time work have flexible schedules, like working from home, only women expect to use the flexibility to meet additional demands at home, while men may "use it to enhance their work performance and get ahead, rather than contribute on the home front." A recent study by Ajjan et al. (2020, p. 11) similarly suggests that women typically experience higher WLC than men:

> Our findings show that gender and the presence of children under the age of 18 affect workers' control over time, technology usefulness, and WFH [Working From Home] conflict... Of note, women experience more lack of control over their time and find technology to be less useful than their male counterparts. Also of interest is that women with children at home report much higher WFH conflict and even less control over time than men who have children at home.

This is in contrast with our results in the context of global software development. While the reasons for the differences are open to discussion and debate, we believe that self-selection, which may result from professional orientation and pride, life situation, work ideologies, and the conscious development of abilities to cross work–life boundaries efficiently and frequently, and to multitask between work and home responsibilities, are worth considering for global software development professionals.

Given the "flexibility" that may be perceived by each family member in the absence of the need to get to work or school at a certain time, individuals may decide on their own preferred clocks and rhythms, thereby causing further disorientation in the family. For example, our scenario's college student may have to attend online classes, and even engage in social time with friends while others in the family are asleep, and he may be sleepy or disoriented even during family lunchtime.

Temporally, there could be instances of work time encroaching upon family/personal times, and family times encroaching upon family/personal times, and forming a vicious cycle of time-based distress and conflict. For example, according to Matyszczyk (2021), Microsoft recently found that 52% of its IM messaging was happening "between 6 pm and midnight." A similar situation can occur with respect to place as well, unless the living quarters are large enough to afford each member of the family physical places needed for his/her preferred activities, sometimes independent of the other family members. A recent conversation with a blended family highlighted similar challenges. Given the COVID-induced lockdown, the kids were all back home. While the house they lived in was large, it was not enough to accommodate six kids and the two parents, to the extent that one of the college-going kids was taking the online classes by sitting in the bathtub of one of the bathrooms (the only quiet space in the house). Further, with respect to work–life boundary, the following quote from Atkins (2020) illustrates what frequently happens:

> ... first, there is no excuse or escape from work when colleagues and bosses know you're never more than a quick walk to your workstation. Sure, that diaper might need changing, the pet might be about to relieve themselves on the floor... but who cares? Your boss knows you got that email about that memo, and he knows you're pretty close to your computer. (para. 5)

As many employees are forced to enact the encompassing work ideology, irrespective of what their own ideology is, WLC is bound to shoot up. Furthermore, this can result in role expansion and unplanned role switching, resulting in not only *strain-based* but also *behavior-based* conflict between expectations related to different roles the individual plays: boss at work, and mom to her children at home. For example, her work may expect "emotional restrictedness" while her family members expect "openness" (Greenhaus & Beutell, 1985, p. 82). The competing nature of these two modes of working increases WLC.

The fourth issue is that *knowledge work, whether global or local, is increasingly seeing intensification*. There are at least two reasons for such intensification. First is the general sense of job uncertainty and anxiety due to the shaky economy, the plummeting revenues for companies as well as the dramatic shrinking of the overall labor markets. Atkins (2020), for example, makes the following observation:

> Bosses concerned about a lack of productivity and control over a team of employees working from home are often increasing their workloads and maximizing digital surveillance of their working time to ensure that no one slacks off and that quotas are met. This is borderline sociopathic to impose on employees whose household duties have obviously increased due to being shut in without the benefit of extraneous assistance or escape for mental health, but it's a widespread phenomenon nonetheless. (para. 6)

The second reason is that the so-called flexibility arising from the lack of a clear sense of place and time appropriate for work and the assumption of "always on" has multiplicative effects on demands on employees' time and attention, especially when the work colleagues are distributed around the globe. As we saw in the case study presented in Chapter 4, global work can place a lot of demands, stretching the traditional borders between work and life whose existence is well understood. With the disappearing of these borders, where work time, sleep time, and personal time all overlap with each other and different cycles of activities unfold in the same physical place, it is not difficult to imagine a situation that would result in extreme strain and, consequently, very high WLC.

Toward a Participative Approach to Border Management

Before we wrap up this chapter with a discussion of an approach for managing WLC in the current situation, it is important to revisit some of the broad findings from our studies:

1. Managing WLC is important for the well-being of individuals. It is also important for organizations that would like to have a committed and healthy workforce that is not prone to incessant turnover.
2. In the context of IT work, especially those conducted in distributed settings, some level of WLC is inevitable; thus, the focus going forward should not be on how to eliminate it, but to manage demands of the work domain effectively by harmonizing it with the work ideology and other life circumstances of the employee.
3. Individuals can have very different ideologies regarding their work and life (e.g., encompassing, compartmentalized, and overlapping), which result in very different needs and expectations. Therefore, expecting universal policies or initiatives to work in organizations is likely to lead to disappointment.
4. WLC, and indeed the work–life ideology, and several personal circumstances of the individual are dependent on his/her phase of life.
5. Individuals are embedded within a constellation of stakeholders including but not limited to work, supervisors, family, technology, and community. Successful management of WLC requires creating/maintaining a reasonable level of alignment among these many elements of the constellation.
6. Owing to the many demands associated with different components of the constellation, individuals have to constantly match the demands with the available resources as they constantly cross borders

of their work and nonwork-related domains. Since these borders might differ in their flexibility, permeability, temporality, and many other dimensions, the objective is to strive to make the "crossing" as seamless as possible.

7. The COVID world has created additional "border-related restrictions" (sometimes radically changing the time–space configurations of work and life) and has resulted in increased violations with respect to one's WLC ideology and environment (Kreiner et al., 2009). For example, individuals holding a separation perspective are likely to perceive considerable discomfort and high WLC as opposed to those with encompassing perspectives. Moreover, all members of the family are not likely to hold the same perspective, as in our scenario, which can cause further WLC. This calls for a more dynamic and proactive approach to border management.
8. It must also be acknowledged that given the COVID crisis and related lockdowns, border crossers "can't function well *without accommodation for their family responsibilities*" (Thomason & Williams, 2020, para. 9). Thus, the view of the "idealized worker" who is available 24/7, even if the worker's own work–life perspective is open to or welcomes such arrangements, may not be valid, especially over a time period spanning several months.
9. The COVID situation has also brought about a tension between resources and demands, where the same component of the constellation which was once a resource may be acting as a demand (e.g., technology, initially an enabler of policies such as work from home, is now creating challenges such as exhaustion, constant connectivity, sleeplessness, to name only a few). Thus, WLC will need to be managed with an eye toward the demand-resource tension across the relationships in the work and life domains.

As mentioned earlier, the literature on WLC and WLC-related policies or initiatives in organizations has generally pursued a one-size-fits-all approach. Policies are typically put together for "everyone" in the organization, and the onus is on "individual border crossers" to embrace it and utilize it. Clearly, our constellation view suggests that such universal approaches are not likely to be very effective; consequently, we call for adopting a more collaborative approach to border management. Taking inspiration from how agencies across the world collaboratively work toward managing national borders (Doyle, 2010), we want to leave our readers with the notion of "participative border management" that is consistent with Border Theory, introduced in Chapter 1, as a way to address WLC challenges.

Below, we discuss three different tactics for managing WLC inspired by the collaborative border management perspective (Doyle, 2010): (1) border construction, (2) border reconfiguration, and (3) border patrolling. Each of these tactics will require the active participation of all/many of the elements in the focal individual's constellation.

Border Construction

A first step toward border construction is that key human stakeholders within a constellation need to acknowledge that, in most cases, some sort of border, albeit of different strengths (i.e., flexibility and permeability) depending on the variety of factors including the work–life ideologies of relevant individuals, needs to be created. Further, everyone concerned should also be committed to maintain, protect, and manage this border effectively. Such borders can be physical and/or temporal. Going back to the scenario we discussed earlier, it could mean that the parent who works as the end-user-tech-support (referred to as Parent 2), based on consultation with family members, supervisor, and friends, may block certain times in his calendar to ensure time with family. He may also consider *constructing physical office space at home* (a physical border) which would be a signal to the rest of the family that it is a border not to be crossed while Parent 2 is at work, thereby giving him uninterrupted work time during regular hours. Temporal borders can be created by blocking certain communication channels, such as voice calls, emails, or IMs at certain times of the day.

From an organization's point of view, it is important to similarly recognize the perceptions and ideologies regarding borders that the two parents hold and to construct them with the individual and his/her environmental circumstances in mind. The constellation view highlights the point that borders for each individual crosser may need tailoring based on a number of dynamic forces, which might include work situation, technology, ideology, and family demands. Going forward, we believe that this difficult task of matching and optimizing a range of border-related variables could potentially benefit from the use of *AI-based tools* (Rai et al., 2019) that can help generate such tailored borders and border management steps for individuals.

Border Reconfiguration

One of the core messages that has emerged from our studies and is further accentuated by the COVID crisis, is the fact that borders that individuals/organizations construct are not static and need constant adjustment. Hirschi et al. (2019) alert us to the fact that without these reconfigurations or revisions, individuals might just "abandon" their course—which, in the context of WLC, may be manifested in the erosion of borders, or in individuals feeling abandoned and unsupported by the relevant border keepers. In the context of our scenario, Parent #1 (located in North America) often has to work on technical problem-solving with her colleagues in Asia. This is likely to occur during hours that may typically be considered family time, and can go on beyond the time anticipated. Given that she has been the acknowledged organizer of family meals and childcare, during such times, her borders might need to be dynamically reconfigured, and one of the other members of her constellation (say, Parent #2) might need to fill her home role temporarily.

While technology has been viewed as an enabler of work-from-home situations, especially during the COVID crisis, it is an important non-human stakeholder in the WLC constellation, and can play a significant role in accentuating or mitigating WLC. Parent #1, for example, spends a significant amount of time during her work hours on Zoom calls with clients and her local and global team members. As mentioned earlier, the constant use of Zoom has many detrimental effects such as eye strain and exhaustion, to name only two. Parent #1 and her organization (in partnership), in an effort to ameliorate such a situation, may consider scheduling meetings on Zoom intermittently throughout the day, often following up over audio only, or reorganizing work into modular chunks so as to avoid the need for synchronous meetings and reduce the level of interdependence in collaborative work especially, but not limited to, work across time zones (see Chapter 4).

Border Patrolling

A very important aspect of border management is patrolling the border and ensuring that few violators sneak through beyond the agreed level of flexibility and permeability. While in a traditional management scenario the role of border patrolling is usually the responsibility of a specific border keeper, in the case of participative border management, we believe that this responsibility lies with each member of the constellation. One aspect of minimizing violation is to create a "virtual border" (Doyle, 2010) where possible violations that can occur are anticipated ahead of time. Going back to our scenario, this may involve a candid conversation among the family members. Parents #1 and #2 can then negotiate with their respective organizations regarding what their borders are, when it is likely to need greater flexibility, when it can change in its permeability, and derive effective strategies to manage such spillovers or incursions across borders when they arise. For example, Parent #2 might consider ensuring that his work mobile phone is set on "off mode" and not "vibrate mode" after regular work hours so that technology truly protects his boundaries during his time with friends and family. The extent of boundary incursions through the mobile phone may be recorded and could be periodically reviewed and acted upon, as part of border patrolling.

Organizations can also focus on using technology and data to segment employees, and monitor those carefully who are at high risk of being repeat violators of others' borders. In border management terminology, such a strategy is termed as "intelligence driven risk management" (McLinden et al., 2011). Similar to the point mentioned above in the previous paragraph, this could involve keeping logs or data of how many after-hour meetings, emails, and reports an individual border crosser has participated in (or worked on), and creating weekly reports on such activities, can help managers stay ahead of identifying potential violators, helping to manage WLC. For an individual for whom such violations are deemed unacceptable, this can take the form of ensuring that meetings scheduled are completed by 5 pm and that emails are not sent or accepted after 5 pm., unless there is an emergency. The idea here is to manage expectations so that no border crosser feels obliged to answer emails, calls, or attend Zoom calls at any cost. An approach to managing this is to remember that "Tech is a Trade" (https://humanetech.com/digital-wellbeing-covid/). What are organizations trading for the 24/7 connectivity of employees? For an increasing number of people around the world, if the answer is employees' well-being, then perhaps it is not worth investing in. About six years ago, the German company, Daimler devised a strategy where emails would be automatically deleted for an employee if they were on holiday. The sender would then be provided with other suggested alternate employees to contact, along with email addresses, in case the email needed immediate attention (Barrett, 2019).

While we are not suggesting such drastic measures, being conscious of demands that checking and responding to emails place on employees, can be helpful in border patrolling.

Another strategy might be what Telenor in Scandinavia termed as "workfulness," an effort at promoting "tech-free meetings and email-free hours" (Barrett, 2019). While tech-free meetings might be challenging to implement in the midst of COVID, alternating between intrusive (video) and less-intrusive (audio or text) technologies, and email-free working hours can be a step toward protecting borders and preventing border violations. Yet another option might be to engage in "digital detox" programs where outside consultants can develop tailored strategies to help employees ensure that "they were in control of the technology rather than it being in control of them" (Barrett, 2019, para. 30).

To conclude, we reiterate that ensuring the balance between work and life through border management is a *multidimensional optimization problem*. Neither a simple manipulation of a few known variables nor a one-size-fits-all organizational initiative is likely to be helpful in managing WLC for all employees. A truly participatory approach, combined with a view that "we are all in this together" can help, especially as we deal with the pandemic and a global lockdown, and as we seek to emerge from it. For a long time, Information Systems scholars have sought to harness technology for instrumental benefits such as efficiency, productivity, and profitability; yet, as Sarker et al. (2019) have observed, for organizational success to be sustainable, technology needs to be harnessed to pursue not just instrumental goals *or* humanistic goals pertaining to human well-being in isolation, but to pursue both together, in a synergistic fashion, with humanistic outcomes contributing to instrumental outcomes and vice versa, recursively. Technology-mediated distributed work is here to stay, and we all need to work together to ensure that the promised productivity gains do not get individuals in a vicious cycle of a life devoid of any balance. Instead, we need to work toward a harmony between our work and life, with the satisfaction of knowing that we have contributed meaningfully to the domain of work, and, at the same time, of celebrating the experience of life that has been lived well.

References

Ajjan, H., Abujarour, S., Fedorowicz, J., & Owens, D. (2020). *Working from home during the COVID-19 crisis: A closer look at gender differences*. International Research Workshop on Women, IS, and Grand Challenges.

Atkins, D. (2020). Working from home should promote work-life balance, not destroy it. *Washington Monthly*. https://washingtonmonthly.com/2020/04/25/working-from-home-should-promote-work-life-balance-not-destroy-it/. Accessed December 28, 2020.

Barrett, P. (2019). Digital wellbeing: Caring for employees in an 'always on' culture. *HRZone*. https://www.hrzone.com/lead/future/digital-wellbeing-caring-for-employees-in-an-always-on-culture. Accessed December 28, 2020.

Brod, C. (1984). *Technostress: The human cost of the computer revolution*. Addison Wesley, MA.

Califf, C. B., Sarker, S., & Sarker, S. (2019). The bright and dark sides of Technostress: A mixed-methods study involving healthcare IT. *MIS Quarterly, 44*(2), 809–856.

Carlson, J. R., & Zmud, R. W. (1999). Channel expansion theory and the experiential nature of media richness perceptions. *The Academy of Management Journal., 42*(2), 153–217.

Dizik, A. (2020). How to work from home with your kids during coronavirus. *BBC*. https://www.bbc.com/worklife/article/20200401-how-to-work-from-home-with-your-kids-during-coronavirus. Accessed December 28, 2020.

Doyle, T. (2010). Collaborative border management. *World Customs Journal, 4*(1), 15–21.

Greenhaus, J. H., & Beutell, N. J. (1985). Sources of conflict between work and family roles. *Academy of Management Review, 10*(1), 76–88.

Haney, C. (2001). *From prison to home: The effect of incarceration and reentry on children, families, and communities*. The psychological impact of incarceration: Implications for post-prison adjustment. https://aspe.hhs.gov/basic-report/psychological-impact-incarceration-implications-post-prison-adjustment. Accessed December 28, 2020.

Hirschi, A., Shockley, K. M., & Zacher, H. (2019). Achieving work-family balance: An action regulation model. *Academy of Management Review, 44*(1), 150–171.

Jiang, M. (2020). The reason Zoom calls drain your energy. *BBC*. https://www.bbc.com/worklife/article/20200421-why-zoom-video-chats-are-so-exhausting. Accessed December 28, 2020.

Kreiner, G. E., Hollensbe, E. C., & Sheep, M. L. (2009). Balancing borders and bridges: Negotiating the work-home interface via boundary work tactics. *Academy of Management Journal, 52*(4), 704–730.

Leslie, L. M., King, E. B., & Clair, J. A. (2019). Work-life ideologies: The contextual basis and consequences of beliefs about work and life. *Academy of Management Review, 44*(1), 72–98.

Liang, L. (2020). Life after lockdown: How China went back to work. *BBC*. https://www.bbc.co.uk/worklife/article/20200430-is-china-going-back-to-normal-coronavirus-covid-19. Accessed December 28, 2020.

Lufkin, B. (2020). How to work from home, the right way. *BBC*. https://www.bbc.com/worklife/article/20200312-coronavirus-covid-19-update-work-from-home-in-a-pandemic. Accessed December 28, 2020.

Matyszczyk, C. (2021). Microsoft revealed the latest truths about working from home. One is truly disturbing. *Technically Incorrect*. https://www.zdnet.com/article/microsoft-revealed-the-latest-truths-about-working-from-home-one-is-truly-disturbing/. Accessed April 5, 2021.

McLinden, G., Fanta, E., Widdowson, D., & Doyle, T. (Eds.). (2011). *Border management modernization*. The World Bank.

Nemko, M. (2020). Happier in the COVID-19 lockdown? *Psychology Today*. https://www.psychologytoday.com/us/blog/how-do-life/202005/happier-in-the-covid-19-lockdown.

Perrigino, M. B., Dunford, B. B., & Wilson, K. S. (2018). Work–family backlash: The "dark side" of work–life balance (WLB) policies. *Academy of Management Annals, 12*(2), 600–630.

Rai, A., Constantinides, P., & Sarker, S. (2019). Editor's comments: Next-generation digital platforms: Toward human–AI hybrids. *MIS Quarterly, 43*(1), iii–x.

Ragu-Nathan T. S., Tarafdar M., Ragu-Nathan B. S., Tu Q. (2008). The consequences of technostress for end users in organizations: Conceptual development and empirical validation. *Information Systems Research, 19*(4), 417–433.

Sarker, S., & Sahay, S. (2004). Implications of space and time for distributed work: An interpretive study of US-Norwegian systems development teams. *European Journal of Information Systems, 13*(1), 3–20.

Sarker, S., Chatterjee, S., Xiao, X., & Elbanna, A. (2019). The sociotechnical perspective as an 'axis of cohesion' for the IS discipline: Recognizing its historical legacy and ensuring its continued relevance. *MIS Quarterly, 43*(3), 695–719.

Sarker, S., Xiao, X., Sarker, S., & Ahuja, M. (2012). Managing work-life balance of mobile technology-enabled IT workers: Perspectives and strategies. *MIS Quarterly Executive*, 143–157.

Short, J., Williams, E., & Christie, B. (1976). *The social psychology of telecommunications*. Wiley.

Thomason, B., & Williams, H. (2020) What will work-life balance look like after the pandemic? *Harvard Business Review*. https://hbr.org/2020/04/what-will-work-life-balance-look-like-after-the-pandemic.

Wayne, J. H., Matthews, R., Crawford, W., & Casper, W. J. (2019). Predictors and processes of satisfaction with work–family balance: Examining the role of personal, work, and family resources and conflict and enrichment. *Human Resource Management, 59*(1), 25–42.

Appendix 1

Overview

In this appendix, we provide details about the interviews that we have used in the book. Given that the book is a compilation of different studies undertaken over a period of time, the extent of detail available in different datasets is not uniform. Nevertheless, they should give the reader a sense of the individuals whose voices have shaped our perspectives.

For Chapter 1, we drew upon the entire set of interviews (see Tables A.1, A.2, and A.3). For Chapters 2 and 3, we primarily drew upon a subset of interviews pertaining to offshoring (Tables A.1 and A.3). For Chapter 4, we drew upon interviews conducted for the GLOBCOM case (Table A.1). For Chapter 5, we drew upon the interviews with IT professionals and consultants regarding their experiences with mobile device use.

Methodological Overview for the GLOBCOM Case (Primarily for Chapter 4, but Also Used in Chapters 1–3)

Given the paucity of literature on work–life balance issues, and the "emotional" nature of the topic (Domagalski, 1999), we used the "interpretive case study methodology" (e.g., Walsham, 1995, 2006; Sarker et al., 2018) to guide the collection and analysis of data. Data collection primarily

S. Sarker et al., *Navigating Work and Life Boundaries*,
https://doi.org/10.1007/978-3-030-72759-8

Table A.1 Interview details[a]

Respondent details	*Based in*	*Primary role*	*Number of formal meetings/interviews*	*Other informal interactions*
Head of a Division	US	Top Mgmt.	2 interviews; also 1 meeting in a group	None
Director of a Division	US	Top Mgmt.	2 interviews; also 1 meeting in a group	None
Manager #1	US	Project Mgmt.	1	None
Manager #2	US	Project Mgmt.	2	None
Manager #3	US	Project Mgmt.	2 (1 of them on telephone)	Lunch meetings; other interactions
Manager #4	US	Project Mgmt.	2	None
Manager #5	US	Project Mgmt.	1	None
Manager #6	US	Project Mgmt.	1	None
Manager #7	US	Project Mgmt.	1	None
Manager #8	US	Project Mgmt.	None	1 (telephone)
Manager #9	US	Project Mgmt.	None	1 (telephone)
Designer #1	US	Technical Architect	1	None
Consultant #1	US	Development	1	None
Junior Developer	US	Development	1	None
Manager #10	US	Process Improvement Manager	1	None
Senior Staff	US	Staff, Coordination	1	Several interactions
Senior Developer	US; in the past in India	Development/Tech. Advisor	1	None
Manager #11	US; in the past in India	Project Mgmt.	1	None
Two other employees	US	N.A.	None	1 lunch meeting
Manager #12	India	Project Mgmt.	1 (interviewed during visit to the US)	None
Manager #13	India	Project Mgmt.	1 (by telephone)	1 lunch meeting in the US during visit

[a]The titles of some of the interviewees have been modified to disguise the identities of the respondents

involved semi-structured interviews with several organizational members involved in information systems development (ISD) in different capacities in the offshore insourcing setting. Interviews were conducted over a number of years in mid 2000s, with over 20 respondents, including those in top management, project management, and technical roles; further, we interviewed individuals from both onshore and offshore locations (see Table A.1).

Methodological Overview for the Study on the Use of Mobile Devices (Primarily for Chapter 5, but Also Used in Chapter 1)

This article is based on data collected between 2009 and 2012 as part of a larger project, partially funded by the National Science Foundation, an independent US Federal agency. We sought to investigate work–life balance issues of IT professionals (especially those engaged in distributed work) in six countries. At different points in the project, we interviewed around 60 workers at different levels (ranging from analyst to vice-president) in a variety of companies, including Adobe, Boeing, BP, Hewlett-Packard, Microsoft (multiple countries), IBM, LG, Nokia, KPMG, Deloitte, Slalom Consulting, PricewaterhouseCoopers, and a Hitachi joint-venture company. For this article, we focused on the use of mobile technologies and their impact on WLB based on 21 of the larger set of interviews. The demographic information on these 21 interviewees is provided below.

Our primary source of data was the unstructured and semi-structured interviews we conducted (see Table A.2).Our conversations with respondents on mobile technologies and WLB implications were guided by the following broad questions:

1. *What is the nature of your role? (within your organization, your group). What is the nature of tasks you are mainly engaged in?*
2. *Do you use mobile devices in your daily work? If so, how?*
3. *How does the use of mobile devices impact your work?*
4. *In your opinion, what is the relationship between work and personal life? What is your definition of work–life balance? (part of, opposed to, as life, tool for)*

Table A.2 Interview details

Interviewee	*Position/responsibility*	*Industry*	*Gender*	*Country*
1	Project Manager	Telecoms	M	Finland
2	VP	Consulting	M	Korea
3	Senior Manager	Consulting	M	Korea
4	Partner	Consulting	F	Korea
5	Manager	Software Development	M	Denmark
6	Desk Manager; Testing	Software Development	F	India
7	IT Documentation Specialist	Consulting	F	India
8	Internal Installation and Licensing	Software Development	M	India
9	Former CIO	Health Care	M	U.S.
10	Senior Consultant	Consulting	M	U.S.
11	Director	Consulting	F	U.S.
12	Senior Manager	Software Development	F	U.S.
13	Manager	Aerospace	F	U.S.
14	Senior Manager	Consulting	F	U.S.
15	Self-employed	Web Development	M	U.S.
16	Project Manager	Consulting	M	U.S.
17	Senior Program Manager	Software Development	M	U.S.
18	Product Manager	Software Development	M	U.S.
19	Contractor	Consulting	F	U.S.
20	Software Engineer	Software Development	M	U.S.
21	System Security Administrator	Higher Education	F	U.S.

5. *Do you see people around you who have different perceptions of the work–life relationship?*
6. *Does the use of mobile devices for work-related purposes impact your personal life? If so, how?*
7. *Do you use mobile devices in your personal life? If so, how?*
8. *Do you have some suggestions or recommendations for mobile device designers?*
9. *Do you have some suggestions or recommendations for your company about employees' use of mobile devices?*
10. *Do you have any concerns about work–life balance?*
11. *What other factors influence your work–life balance?*

However, there were some variations across the interviews in terms of the issues discussed. This variation was in part due to the diverse set of research questions we were seeking to address in the larger study, the responsibilities and experiences of our respondents, and the evolution of our own understanding of the WLB phenomenon over time.

Finally, our data analysis approach can be characterized as "interpretive," meaning that we sought to develop a holistic understanding of the interviews and to portray the perspectives of our respondents within a coherent framework.

Additional Interviews (Used in Chapters 1–3)

We also conducted some additional interviews with professionals who were involved with some form of distributed work, typically offshoring (see Table A.3).

Table A.3 Additional interview details

Interviewee	*Position/responsibility*	*Gender*	*Country*
1	Program manager, Development team, Requirements & specifications	F	Denmark
2	Supply chain management, Manufacturing team, Program management	M	Denmark
3	Software production planning, Consumer experience planning	M	Denmark
4	Technical lead	M	India
5	Manager, Design Jet Printers	M	India
6	Desk manager, master system (testing)	F	India
7	Lab services and solutions group	M	India
8	Engineering group member	F	India
9	Global services, internal organizational analysis (HR-like)	M	India
10	Senior technical lead, software testing	M	India
11	Product manager (from engineering and development to release)	M	India
12	HR business partner team lead	F	India
13	Sr. Staff firmware engineer	M	US

(continued)

Table A.3 (continued)

Interviewee	*Position/responsibility*	*Gender*	*Country*
14	Sr. messaging administrator, application development	M	US
15	Software engineer	M	US
16	Contractor, IT services & consulting	F	US
17	Application development team	M	US
18	HR & Recruitment Manager	M	India
19	Not Available	M	India
20	Not Available	F	India
21	Not Available	M	India
22	Not Available	M	India
23	Manager, community help and learning (i.e., technical publication partner)	M	India
24	Manager, engineering, software development & architectural lead	M	India
25	Internal installation and licensing	M	India
26	Product documentation development and design	F	India
27	Six Sigma manager	M	India

Appendix 2

See Table A.4.

Overview of the Literature Review on WLB/WLC

In order to understand the state of current research on the topic, we searched both Google scholar and Sociological abstracts (via Proquest) using the terms "work-life balance," work-life conflict," and "work-family conflict." Given a large number of results, we narrowed down the search to studies from the year 1990, and given the still large number, we then created a subset of those studies based on those that have been cited over 100 times. We then screened those studies to assess the relevance, and we provide a representative sample of those studies in Table A.5a.

In our next phase of the review, we searched for studies with the terms "information technology and work-life conflict" and "information technology and work-life balance." This review is in Table A.5b.

S. Sarker et al., *Navigating Work and Life Boundaries*,
https://doi.org/10.1007/978-3-030-72759-8

Table A.4 A review of the literature on Border Theory

Authors and year	*Empirical examination?*	*Major tenets*
Clark (2000)	No	People are border crossers who make transitions between the "world of work" and the "world of family" on a daily basis The proposed theory also helps to understand the interactions these border crossers have with their work environment and their family environment, and how these interactions create conflict within their work-family roles, and how balance may be achieved
Clark (2002)	Yes Survey of 151 employees in the Indian reservation (Nez Perce Indians)	Border Theory was used at a meta level with the author examining the effect of two psychological states of the border crossers, that is, their sense of work community and their sense of control as mediating variables between personal/work factors and work/family conflict Results highlight that border crossers' sense of community and sense of control at work mediate the relationship among four personal/work factors
Desrochers and Saergent (2004)	No It is primarily a review of existing literature on Border Theory	The authors emphasized the difference between border and boundary theory Both Border Theory and boundary theory have good potential for understanding work-family balance and conflict. Border Theory emphasizes the transition between work and family domains, and takes on a broader view of borders, with "borders encompassing not only the psychological categories" but also tangible characteristics such as time, place, people associated with work, etc.

(continued)

Table A.4 (continued)

Authors and year	*Empirical examination?*	*Major tenets*
Bennett et al. (2006)	Yes Survey of individual employees of municipal departments and other independent businesses	Life-to-work stress and drinking norms affects at-risk drinking with co-workers which affects at-risk drinking Border Theory was used at a meta level, with the authors positing that drinking with co-workers can be viewed as "existing in the border zone" of work and life, therefore creating fuzzy borders
Lambert et al. (2006)	Yes Survey of employees in a Biotechnology firm	The model tested was based "partially" on Border Theory, and that too, Border Theory was used at the meta level. Generic variables such as central participation, supportive communication, and life satisfaction, were tested on work-family conflict, and the effect of work-family conflict on job satisfaction. No significant effect was found between work-family conflict and job satisfaction, but there was a significant inverse relationship between work-family conflict and life satisfaction. Central participation was seen as an important variable
Cowan and Hoffman (2007)	Yes An exploratory qualitative study to examine the definition and types of flexibility affecting work-life balance	The authors concluded that flexibility, an important dimension of Border Theory, in the context of work-life balance can be of three types: time flexibility, space (both physical and mental) flexibility, evaluation flexibility, and compensation flexibility
Donald and Linington (2008)	Yes Survey of 92 managers from a large financial institution in Gauteng	Border Theory was used at a meta level only, with authors positing that border crossers and their characteristics have an effect on their transitioning The study focused on the effect of gender role orientation, and other border crosser characteristics such as marital status, on work-life conflict. Results indicated that gender role orientation does not affect work-family conflict

Table A.5a A review of the broader literature on WLB/WLC

Citation	*Context Studied*	*Key antecedents*	*Key consequences*	*Operationalization of Work-Life Balance*	*Findings (demographic and role variables underlined)*	*Category of Variable as Per Border Theory*
Aryee (1992)	Married professional women from dual-career families	Role stressors	3 types of work-family conflict namely, job—spouse, job—parent, and job—homemaker; Effect of these conflicts on well-being and work outcome measures	Items measuring WFC and FWC	Women experience moderate levels of each of these types of conflicts and work roles stressors significantly affected job-spouse and job-homemaker conflict	*Border Crosser's characteristics*
Higgins and Duxbury (1992)	Focus on the differences in work-life conflict between dual-career men and traditional career men	Quality of work and family life, dual career versus traditional career	Work-family conflict and family-work conflict; Effect of WFC and FWC on life satisfaction	Items measuring WFC was developed by drawing on the Job related Tension index from Kahn et al. (1964)	Strong positive relationship between work and family conflict for dual-career (DC) men than traditional career (TC) men; Also, results indicated that DC men experienced greater work-family conflict due to work and not family responsibilities, and that they receive less support from their work environments	*Border Crosser's characteristics*

Citation	*Context Studied*	*Key antecedents*	*Key consequences*	*Operationalization of Work-Life Balance*	*Findings (demographic and role variables underlined)*	*Category of Variable as Per Border Theory*
Rice et al. (1992)	Americans engaged in Paid employment of over 20 hours per week	Work-nonwork conflict composed of both work-family conflict and work-leisure conflict	Quality of nonwork-life and Quality of work life as assessed through family satisfaction, leisure satisfaction, and job satisfaction; Effect of QNWL and QWL on overall quality of life	Two items measuring work-family conflict and work-leisure conflict	Work-family conflict and work-leisure conflict affected job satisfaction and leisure satisfaction; WFC also affected family satisfaction; Three types of satisfaction affected global life satisfaction	*Conflict in crossing borders*
Duxbury et al. (1994)	Canadian public sector employees and private sector employees from large global organizations	Gender, family structure (such as single parents or not), and perceived control over work situation	Work-family conflict	WFc operationalized as role overload, interference from work-to-family, and interference from family-to-work	Women experienced more role overload, and more interference from family-to-work and also work-to-family; Single parents did not show higher role overload or interference from family-to-work; Those with more control over their work situation showed less role overload and interference	*Border Crosser's characteristics*

(continued)

Table A.5a (continued)

Citation	*Context Studied*	*Key antecedents*	*Key consequences*	*Operationalization of Work-Life Balance*	*Findings (demographic and role variables underlined)*	*Category of Variable as Per Border Theory*
Thomas and Ganster (1995)	Health care professionals	Organizational family supportive variables such as dependent services, schedule flexibility, supervisory support, among others	Work-family support; Effect of WFC on strain outcomes such as satisfaction, absenteeism, and health factors such as blood pressure, cholesterol, etc.	Measure of WFC was adapted from Greenhaus et al. (1983)	Flexibility of schedule and supervisory support had either indirect effects (through control) or direct effects on WFC; WFC also reduced some of the health concerns, and had significant effects on job satisfaction	*Border keeper's characteristics*
Parasuraman et al. (1996)	Small business owners in the US	Psychological involvement in work and family life roles, autonomy, spouse instrumental	Work-family conflict and family-work conflict; Effect of WFC and FWC on life stress and career satisfaction	Measures of both WFC and FWC	WFC leads to heightened life stress and FWC negatively affects career dissatisfaction; Psychological involvement has no effect on time commitment but affects WFC and FWC, and autonomy negatively affects FWC	*Border crosser's and Border keeper's characteristics*
Tompson and Werner (1997)	Working individuals enrolled in MBS program	Inter-role conflict	Job satisfaction, organizational commitment, and citizenship behaviors	Inter-role conflict was assessed through a matrix that captured different types of roles that an individual plays from employee to care giver	Role conflicts that exist between work and non-work roles affect organizational citizenship behaviors, and organizational commitment mediates this relationship	*Permeability of the border at a broad level*

Citation	*Context Studied*	*Key antecedents*	*Key consequences*	*Operationalization of Work-Life Balance*	*Findings (demographic and role variables underlined)*	*Category of Variable as Per Border Theory*
Kinnunen and Mauno (1998)	Working men and women in four organization in Finland	Family domain characteristics, and work domain characteristics such as whether it's a full-time job, poor leadership relations, etc.	Work-family conflict and family-work conflict	Items measuring WFC and FWC	No gender difference in the level of WFC or FWC experienced; The WFC had a negative effect on occupational well-being, and FWC had a negative effect on family well-being	***Border crosser's and border keeper's characteristics***
Aryee et al. (1999)	Chinese parents in dual-earner households in HongKong	Role stressors, workload, interrole conflict	Work-family conflict, and family-work conflict; Effect of WFC and FWC on life satisfaction, and job satisfaction	Items developed by authors	Work overload was related to both WFC and FWC; Emotion focused coping helped create positive life satisfaction while both emotion and problem-focused coping helped in job satisfaction	***Border crosser's and Border keeper's characteristics; permeability of the border***
Carlson and Perrewe (1999)	Employees in the Department of State in the US	Work-role conflict, work time demands, work role ambiguity, work social support, family-role conflict, family time demands, family role ambiguity, and family social support	Work-family conflict	Items of WFC developed by the authors by adapting from other scales	Work-family conflict was affected by role ambiguity (both work and family), time demands, and role conflict. Work social support and family social support did not have a direct effect on WFC but indirectly through the role-based variables	***Border Keeper's characteristics***

(continued)

Table A.5a (continued)

Citation	*Context Studied*	*Key antecedents*	*Key consequences*	*Operationalization of Work-Life Balance*	*Findings (demographic and role variables underlined)*	*Category of Variable as Per Border Theory*
Hill et al. (2001)	Employees in IBM though focus was not only on the IT workers	Demographic variables such as gender, martial status, preschoolers in the family, workload, and flex schedule	Work-life balance; Effect of WLB on other variables not studied	Five item measure of WLB developed by the authors	Gender did not affect WLB, work load negatively affected WLB, and flexibility positively affected WLB	*Border crosser's characteristics, and flexibility* of the border
Parasuraman and Simmers (2001)	Working graduate students and professionals in continuing education in the US	Work role characteristics such as employment types, autonomy, flexibility, time commitment, and job involvement, and family structure such as parental demands, family involvement	Work-family conflict; Effect of WFC on job satisfaction, career satisfaction, family satisfaction, and life stress	Measure of both time-based and strain-based work conflict adapted from previous research	Employment type has a strong effect on WFC with business owners or those self-employed experiencing more conflict; Similarly, other work-role characteristics also had strong effects on WFC	*Border crosser's characteristics, border keeper's characteristics, and flexibility* of the border

Citation	*Context Studied*	*Key antecedents*	*Key consequences*	*Operationalization of Work-Life Balance*	*Findings (demographic and role variables underlined)*	*Category of Variable as Per Border Theory*
Aryee et al. (2005)	Working individuals from different organizations in India	Personality characteristics such as neuroticism and optimism, gender, personal and work overload, personal and work involvement, and work social support and family support	Work-life conflict; Effect of work-life conflict on job satisfaction, and organizational commitment	16-item scale of work-family balance from Grzywacz and Marks (2000)	Reaffirmed prior understanding that work-family balance may be conceptualized as both work to family and family to work, and can be both conflict oriented or facilitative; Family support helped in the facilitation, but <u>gender</u> or personality did not have strong effects; Neuroticism and work involvement added to work-family conflict. Work family facilitation positively affected job satisfaction and commitment	*Border crosser's and Border Keeper's characteristics*
Ilies et al. (2007)	Employees of a large mid-western university	Work load, affect at work, and affect at home	Work-family conflict; Effect of WFC on social activity with family	Items measuring WFC taken from Kopelman, Greenhaus, and Connolly (1983)	Workload and affect at work added to work-life conflict, which also negatively affected social activity with family	*Border Keeper's characteristics*

(continued)

Table A.5a (continued)

Citation	*Context Studied*	*Key antecedents*	*Key consequences*	*Operationalization of Work-Life Balance*	*Findings (demographic and role variables underlined)*	*Category of Variable as Per Border Theory*
Premeaux et al. (2007)	Working professionals from different organizations within the southern US	Job autonomy, perceived work-family culture, availability of FFPs, family support, and number of children	Work-family conflict and family-work conflict; Effect of WFC and FWC on satisfaction, affective commitment and continuing commitment	Work-family conflict measured by adapted scale of Carlson et al. (2000)	Job autonomy did not affect WFC, and neither did the availability of FFPs; However, family support had a mitigating effect on conflict, and the number of children increased WFC. Finally, WFC positively affected continuing commitment, and did not affect any of the other outcome variables	*Border Keeper's characteristics*
Valcour (2007)	Employees of a large telecommu-nications company in the US	Work related characteristics such as work hours, control over work time, and job complexity; gender was hypothesized to play a moderating relationship	Satisfaction with work-life balance	Satisfaction with WLB was measured with 5 new items	Work hours, job complexity, and control over work time had significant effects on satisfaction with WLB; Gender did not have a moderating effect	*Border crosser's and Border Keeper's characteristics*

Citation	*Context Studied*	*Key antecedents*	*Key consequences*	*Operationalization of Work-Life Balance*	*Findings (demographic and role variables underlined)*	*Category of Variable as Per Border Theory*
Hill et al. (2010)	Employees of IBM in 75 countries	Workplace and schedule flexibility	Work-life Conflict and ability to work long hours	Measure of WLC taken from the IBM Work and Life issues survey	Workplace flexibility benefits employees since ability to work from home reduces their work-life conflict, and also beneficial to businesses since it gives them long working employees. The benefits of workplace flexibility compounds when combined with schedule flexibility	*Flexibility* of the border

Table A.5b A review of literature on WLB/WLC in IS

Citation	*Context studied*	*Key antecedents*	*Key consequences*	*Operationalization of work-life balance*	*Findings (demographic and role variables underlined)*	*Linkage with border theory and other remarks*
Igbaria et al. (1994)	IS employees and members of the Association of Computing Machinery	Demographic variables such as age and job tenure, work experiences such as boundary-spanning activities, role stressors, task characteristics, level of job involvement, and career expectations	Quality of work life as in job satisfaction, career satisfaction, and organizational commitment	No direct measure of work-life conflict or work-life balance; measures of quality of work life taken from the job satisfaction scale, items from Greenhaus et al. (1990) and Porter et al. (1976)	IS professionals demonstrate three different levels of job involvement; The effect of role stressors and other work characteristics on the quality of work life varies with the level of involvement IS employees have	Primarily *Border Crosser's characteristics*; Context is software work, but no nuanced factors related to IT or ISD were identified; No specific focus on distributed work
Ahuja (2002)	Women in IT, and the antecedents of their career choice in IT, career persistence in IT, and career advancement in IT	Work-life conflict and its effect on career choice, persistence, and advancement; several other social and structural factors were also proposed to have an effect	Career choice in IT; Career persistence in IT; and career advancement in IT	N/A	WLC was proposed to negatively affect career choice and career persistence in IT for women; Women in IT were proposed to have higher WLC than men in IT	*Border Crosser's* characteristics; Context is software work, but no nuanced factors related to IT or ISD were identified; No specific focus on distributed work

Citation	*Context studied*	*Key antecedents*	*Key consequences*	*Operationalization of work-life balance*	*Findings (demographic and role variables underlined)*	*Linkage with border theory and other remarks*
Hyman et al. (2003)	Work-life imbalance in call centers and in software work	Perceived task control, job complexity, and perceived centrality of work	Work-life imbalance	Items of strain and time-based conflict from Greenhaus and Beutell (1995), and also some items that assessed tangible extensions of work into non-work life such as extent to which employees had to work during weekends	Differences were noticed among call center employees and software workers in terms of their perceived task control and job characteristics. Further, software employees perceived more blurry lines between work and non-work life than call center employees	*Border crosser and border keeper's characteristics*; Context is software work, but no nuanced factors related to IT or ISD were identified; No specific focus on distributed work
Scholarios and Marks (2004)	Focus on software workers; empirical study conducted in two software organizations in Scotland	Supervisory support, time flexibility, organizational support, and work to non-work spillovers	Trust in organizations; Effect of trust on affective commitment, job satisfaction, and intention to remain in the company	WLB/WLC was not specifically examined; Work to non-work spillover was measured using Greenhaus and Beutell's (1985) scale of time and strain-based conflict	Time flexibility, organizational support, and work-non-work spillovers affected trust in organizations and organizational commitment and satisfaction	*Border keeper's characteristics* and *generic permeability of the border*; Context is software work, but no nuanced factors related to IT or ISD were identified; No specific focus on distributed work

(continued)

Table A.5b (continued)

Citation	*Context studied*	*Key antecedents*	*Key consequences*	*Operationalization of work-life balance*	*Findings (demographic and role variables underlined)*	*Linkage with border theory and other remarks*
Quesenberry and Trauth (2005)	Women in the IT workforce	Asynchronous communication office relationships, and ubiquitous technologies	Work-life balance	N/A; Interview data used	Ubiquitous technologies actually help women address their various needs and roles, and thereby enable the integration of their work and family life, and achieve better balance	Broadly some of the factors can be categorized as part of the *border crosser's* characteristics; Context is software work, but no nuanced factors related to IT or ISD were identified; No specific focus on distributed work
Messersmith (2007)	Focus on the work-life conflict in the IT profession	Time-based conflict strain-based conflict ranging from factors such working long hours, being on-call to role ambiguity as well as individual factors such as high job involvement and motivation	General outcomes of work-life conflict such as organizational commitment	N/A	The author first identified several antecedents of work-life conflict in IT workers, and proposed certain ways to address them such as by introducing family friendly policies, integrating family, leisure and work life by creating more fun environments in the workplace, and introducing socialization tactics for new IT hires	*Border crosser's characteristics*; Context is software work, but no nuanced factors related to IT or ISD were identified; No specific focus on distributed work

Citation	*Context studied*	*Key antecedents*	*Key consequences*	*Operationalization of work-life balance*	*Findings (demographic and role variables underlined)*	*Linkage with border theory and other remarks*
Ahuja et al. (2007)	IT professionals who spend most of their work week away from home at a client site	Perceived work overload, job autonomy, work-family conflict, and fairness of rewards	Work exhaustion and organizational commitment, and effect of them on turnover intention	Work-family conflict items adapted from Adams et al. (1996)	Work-family conflict is an important predictor of work exhaustion, which also has significant effects on turnover intentions; perceived work overload has a strong effect on work-family conflict as well	*Border crosser and border keeper's characteristics;* Context is software work, but no nuanced factors related to IT or ISD were identified; No specific focus on distributed work
Armstrong et al. (2007)	Women in IT working in a Fortune 500 manufacturing firm	Exploratory study; No variables were hypothesized in the beginning	Work-family conflict and voluntary turnover	N/A; Qualitative data from six focus groups were used to develop causal maps surrounding the interaction of work and family responsibilities for women in IT	The authors concluded that several types of loops of relationships exist between managing family responsibilities, workplace schedule flexibility, job quality, and work stress, and that these factors also affected women's career advancement, and turnover	*N/A;* Context is IT work, but no nuanced factors related to IT or ISD were identified; No specific focus on distributed work; Focus on women only

(continued)

Table A.5b (continued)

Citation	*Context studied*	*Key antecedents*	*Key consequences*	*Operationalization of work-life balance*	*Findings (demographic and role variables underlined)*	*Linkage with border theory and other remarks*
Fenner and Renn (2010)	Technology-assisted supplemental work (TASW)	Perceived usefulness of certain technologies and psychological climate was hypothesized to affect TASW, while TASW was hypothesized to positively affect work-family conflict	TASW; Effect of TASW on Work-life conflict	3 items from Kopelman et al. (1983) and two from Frone et al. (1992)	TASW was seen as a variant of distributed work, and perceived usefulness of technology and psychological climate were seen to affect it. TASW was seen to positively affect WLC, and time management moderated this relationship	*N/A*; Context is software work, but no nuanced factors related to IT or ISD were identified; No specific factors related to distributed work was identified
Sarker et al. (2010)	IT professionals based in India involved in globally-distributed software development	The effect of time difference, frequency of communication, the interaction between frequency of communication and synchronous communication extent, number of distributed locations and the interaction between number of locations and perceived similarity on work-life conflict and Valence toward distributed ISD	WLC and Valence toward distributed ISD	Kopelman et al.'s (1983) scale for WLC; Valence toward distributed ISD	Time Zone difference and the interaction between frequency of communication and synchronous communication extent found to influence WLC; The number of distributed locations and the interaction between number of locations and perceived similarity found to influence Valence	*Temporal borders*; *physical borders*; and *extent of domain members*

Citation	*Context studied*	*Key antecedents*	*Key consequences*	*Operationalization of work-life balance*	*Findings (demographic and role variables underlined)*	*Linkage with border theory and other remarks*
Singh (2010)	Awareness of WLB policies amongst Software professionals in India	N/A	N/A	N/A; WLC or WLB was not specifically assessed; awareness of different organizational policies regarding WLB were assessed	Low levels of general WLB policies amongst software professionals; Specific cultural/religious leave and referral services for employees were perceived as important WLB policies	*N/A*; Context is software work, but no nuanced factors related to IT or ISD were identified; No specific focus on distributed work
Zhao and Rashid (2010)	Knowledge workers of Chinese and Indian origin in a large global bank	Role ambiguity, role conflict, and role overload	Work-life conflict; Effect of WLC on retention	Five items of WLC adapted from Small and Riley (1990)	WLC is an important mediator in the relationship between job-stress related variables such as role ambiguity and role overload, and retention	*Border crosser's characteristics*; Context is software work, but no nuanced factors related to IT or ISD were identified; No specific focus on distributed work
Bohle et al. (2011)	Customer service operators of call centers in Australia	Variability of hours, schedule control, work intensity, employment status, and weekly hours	Work-life conflict; Effect of WLC on chronic fatigue and psychological concerns	WLC measured using items from Bohle and Tilley (1998) and Frone and Yardley (1996)	Work intensity and dissatisfaction with hours affected WLC, and WLC in turn had significant effects on chronic fatigue and several psychological symptoms	*Border crosser's characteristics* and *flexibility* of the border; Context is software work, but no nuanced factors related to IT or ISD were identified; No specific focus on distributed work

(continued)

Table A.5b (continued)

Citation	*Context studied*	*Key antecedents*	*Key consequences*	*Operationalization of work-life balance*	*Findings (demographic and role variables underlined)*	*Linkage with border theory and other remarks*
Valk and Srinivasan (2011)	Women IT professionals in India	No upfront factors were hypothesized	Work-Life balance	N/A; Qualitative interviews used to understand the factors affecting WLB	Role models, role conflict, work-identity, family identity, nature of the IT industry, prioritization of commitments, personal self-management, women friendliness, work-family programs, work-family support received, domestic help, and supervisor and co-worker support all affect work-life balance	*Border crosser and border keeper's characteristics*; Context is software work, but no nuanced factors related to IT or ISD were identified; No specific focus on distributed work

Appendix 3

This appendix offers details regarding the survey and analysis. There is a degree of overlap between what has been discussed in the chapter and what we provide here.

The Sample

In testing our model, we employed a survey of IT professionals involved in GDSD in the United States, the United Kingdom, and India. The United States was chosen because it is the main country of interest for the researchers and engages in the highest amount of distributed software development with other countries. The United Kingdom serves as the IT hub for distributed software development in Europe, and India provides a significant proportion of IT workers for GDSD projects (Robinson & Kalakota, 2004). Furthermore, given our "convergence" perspective (Stohl, 2001), which argues for the absence of cross-country differences in the global, professionalized knowledge-based economy, our primary motive for surveying subjects from three different countries was to ensure that we did not inadvertently introduce bias potentially associated with perspectives from one country only.

The survey was administered by an external organization based on the east coast of the United States that was contracted by the authors, using funds received from a National Science Foundation grant. The organization specializes in conducting large-scale surveys for organizations

S. Sarker et al., *Navigating Work and Life Boundaries*,
https://doi.org/10.1007/978-3-030-72759-8

and research institutions. The primary level of analysis in this study is that of an individual. Thus, the organization was responsible for identifying individual subjects for the survey, given the specifications provided (i.e., sampling criteria) by the authors. Furthermore, the organization was responsible for ensuring that completed surveys were returned, and then the survey participants were appropriately compensated. Our sample may be considered "purposive random sampling" (Venkatesh et al., 2016, p. 446), where a random sample of subjects was chosen from a larger group following a particular criteria (that is, GDSD members from three countries). The criteria provided included ensuring that participants worked in a GDSD environment in some capacity related to software development projects and were located in the United States, the United Kingdom, or India. The organization was paid for the sample, the software, the participant compensation, and their overall services. The final sample consisted of 1,000 GDSD participants.

Measures

We used established scales, wherever possible, for measuring our core constructs.

Even though we utilized adapted versions of the previously validated scales in most cases (see Chapters 2 and 3), many of our adapted measures (except for task interdependency and the item measuring technology diversity) were validated in prior pilot studies of IT professionals working in a GDSD environment in India and Europe. These pilot studies were conducted within a period of approximately two years before the main study. Furthermore, prior to the administration of the survey among the respondents of the current study, the face validity of items was again assessed by selected GDSD experts.

Control Variables

As mentioned earlier, our sample consisted of GDSD participants from the United States, the United Kingdom, and India. Studies highlight that in the context of work–life balance, one might see some variations across these countries. For example, India is a traditional society with strongly defined gender and family roles that come under pressure as a result of globally distributed work (Kumari & Devi, 2013), and thus, we believe that studying GDSD professionals in India in comparison with those in the United States and the United Kingdom can provide interesting national culture-based insights. We note that while it is popularly believed that the United States and the United Kingdom are very similar, recent studies argue that very significant differences do exist between them, especially because employment laws in the United Kingdom are considered more protective of their employees than in the United States (U.S. vs. U.K. Employment Law, 2012).

In a study of the role of management practices in organizations, Bloom et al. (2009) found that the United States had "less generous" work–life balance practices than the United Kingdom. We believe that these differences in the practices can have a bearing on the employees' perspectives surrounding work–life balance. Finally, in the World Values Survey, the United States and the United Kingdom are placed very differently on a number of dimensions including long-term and short-term orientation, with the United Kingdom being seen as long-term while the United States being seen as short-term. In long-term orientation cultures, individuals do not view leisure time to be as important, which we believe can significantly impact how employees will perceive work–life balance and its causes (Hofstede et al., 2010). Incidentally, India's orientation has been found to be highly long-term oriented (Hofstede et al., 2010). Further, India has also been seen as being a "restrained" culture, where leisure is not only less important, but also preferring leisure time can be seen as a negative trait of an individual (Hofstede et al., 2010).

While the countries have differences that could provide an interesting comparison, drawing on more recent literature on culture, we opted to use *country* as a control variable as opposed to an independent or moderating variable. Schwartz (2006, 2014), a leading intercultural scholar, has specifically argued for use of country as a control. He puts forth the argument that, with the globalization of work practices (as in the case of GDSD), this is a more appropriate approach for individual-level data collection. He suggests that while cultural value orientations are appropriate for comparing societal groups to one another, they are not appropriate for characterizing the values of individual people and studying the relationships surrounding individual values and differences. Furthermore, in this study, we adopted a "convergence" perspective to culture—this perspective argues that, for those involved in knowledge work and in the globalized economy, we seldom witness significant cross-cultural differences (Stohl, 2001). This is particularly the case where workers are professionalized as part of a global workforce, as in the case of

GDSD. Consequently, we chose to use the country as a control variable. We believe that the use of country as a control variable also helped remove bias in our data. In an effort to remain open to possible differences with respect to WLC across countries that could exist, GDSD personnel from different countries were included in the study. Finally, while the respondents' perceptions may not be very different based on "culture," individuals in these three locations could have had different specializations and roles in GDSD. Thus, the choice of country as a control variable helped to address this possible bias as well. We coded respondents as 1, 2, or 3 depending on whether they came from India, the United Kingdom, or the United States.

We would like to reiterate that while our study focused on the role of *organizational* and *domain-specific characteristics* on WLC, the traditional literature on WLC has highlighted the role of several individual-related characteristics that tend to play a role on WLC, notable among which is *the effect of gender* and *family structure*, the latter often concerned with dependents (e.g., Greenhaus & Beutell, 1985, Poelmans et al., 2009). We must note that the traditional WLB/WLC literature strongly suggests that gender affects work–life conflict, with women experiencing more conflict than men (e.g., Duxbury & Higgins, 1994, Gutek et al., 1991, Lyonette et al., 2007). An alternative set of studies, however, holds that men experience more conflict than women. Some scholars have argued that "women have been socialized over the generations to the nurturing role of the family. No matter how achievement orientated the woman is" (Gambles et al., 2006, p. 77), she is able to balance these two domains more easily and thus experiences similar levels of conflict as men. We believe professionalization of the GDSD workforce and self-selection to this line of work could contribute to the lack of WLC differences among men and women. In testing our model in Chapter 2, we controlled for both *gender* and whether *individuals take care of dependents*. Such variables are often chosen to be control variables in studies on WLC (e.g., Dierdoff & Ellington, 2008; Lambert et al., 2004). We measured each of these with single items.

Furthermore, since prior experience in working in distributed software development can be drawn on in addressing the challenges of distribution, we also sought to control for participants' *prior experience in GDSD*. Indeed, from our interviews, it appeared that employees with experience in the distributed environment had organized their life accepting and accommodating the incursions of work, while setting aside times for personal and family life. We measured the variable (prior experience in GDSD) by using a single item that asked them to specify the number of years they had worked in distributed IS development.

Finally, in Chapter 2, we controlled for the *role* they played in GDSD. Prior research on work–life balance suggests that the introduction of new forms of work and new "communication technologies enabling constant contact with employees and the need for businesses to cut lead times have led to increased time pressures and intrusion of work into non-work times for managers" (Lyness & Judiesch, 2008, p. 789). This can potentially be more pronounced for those who work in GDSD environments and are in charge of managing the projects across locations and clients. We asked respondents to specify their roles from a given set of options, which we coded as having a primarily technical or a project management/relationship management role.

Among our sample of 1,000 GDSD participants, 500 were from the United States, 251 were from the United Kingdom, and 249 were from India. 767 were males and 233 were females. 345 individuals played a project management-related role, while 655 were in more technical roles. Their average experience in distributed software development was 6.59 years, with a median experience of 5 years. 498 of the respondents indicated that they needed to take care of dependents, while 502 indicated that they did not.

Analysis Techniques

We used SmartPLS 2.0 M3 to analyze our survey data. Our selection of the analysis technique is in line with recent methodological thinking within the IS discipline on the use of partial least squares (PLS) versus other analysis techniques such as regression or SEM (e.g., Gefen et al., 2001, Ringle et al., 2012). Specifically, it has been argued that PLS is more suitable when (1) the study is "data-rich" (Gefen et al., 2011), as in our case, and also (2) uses a number of single-item constructs (given that PLS allows for "unrestricted use of single item constructs"; Ringle et al., 2012, p. vii). Furthermore, Goodhue et al. (2012) argue that PLS is better suited over CB-SEM when the focus is on understanding the nature of the relationships as opposed to the magnitude of those relationships, as in early investigations of a particular phenomenon. We believe this is consistent with the goals of our study. Also, Goodhue et al. (2012)

found that PLS was equivalent to other techniques in terms of power and identifying false positives.

Consistent with prior research using PLS models, we analyzed our model in two stages (e.g., Chin 1998; Bhattacharya & Premkumar, 2004; Gefen & Straub, 2005; Hulland, 1999): the first stage involved "the assessment of the reliability and the validity of the measurement model," and the second stage involved "the assessment of the structural model" (Hulland, 1999, p. 198).

Assessment of the Measurement Model. We ensured the quality of our results and the inferences made from the quantitative study by paying close attention to validities (Venkatesh et al., 2016). Convergent validity was established by satisfying the following three criteria (e.g., Bhattacharya & Premkumar, 2004; Gefen & Straub, 2005; Hulland, 1999). First, all items loaded significantly on their respective constructs, and none of the item loadings were below the cutoff value of 0.503. Second, the composite reliabilities of all constructs were over 0.70. Discriminant validity was established by the Fornell–Larcker test—that is, by ensuring that for each construct, the square root of its AVE exceeded all correlations between that factor and any other construct (Bhattacharya & Premkumar 2004; Fornell & Larcker, 1981; Gefen & Straub, 2005). Thus, overall, our measures demonstrated good psychometric properties (see Table A.6).

Assessment of the Hypothesized Relationships. In the analysis, we controlled for gender, care for dependents, experience in distributed software development, role, and country while assessing the models. As suggested in prior research (e.g., Kock, 2011), in PLS, control variables are included as independent variables as part of the study without hypothesizing for its effect.

We utilized multiple methods to assess common method variance (CMV), which may be considered a concern given that the independent and dependent variables were measured in one survey. First, to ensure that our model does not suffer from CMV, we applied the recommendation of Podsakoff et al. (2003). This included assuring respondents of anonymity. Furthermore, using Harman's single-factor test (Podsakoff et al., 2003), we found that 13 factors emerged with an eigenvalue greater than one, and there was no general factor apparent in the un-rotated factor solution, indicating that common method variance was not a problem. Next, we employed the marker variable approach proposed by Lindell and Whitney (2003), specifically following the guidelines suggested by Ronkko and

Table A.6 Square root of AVEs,[a] composite reliabilities, and correlations

	Construct	*Composite reliability*	*1*	*2*	*3*	*4*	*5*	*6*	*7*	*8*	*9*	*10*	*11*	*12*	*13*	*14*	*15*	*16*	*17*	*18*
1	WLC	.939	**.811**																	
2	Turnover_int	.922	.402	**.865**																
3	Perf	.928	−.021	−.177	**.930**															
4	Org_FFP	.949	−.128	−.159	.172	**.820**														
5	Supv_Supp	.962	−.130	−.240	.295	.590	**.836**													
6	Flex_Sched	.741	.110	−.128	.068	.193	.176	**.716**												
7	Agile_Methods	.962	−.155	−.168	−.026	−.118	−.022	−.031	**.963**											
8	Locational_Disp	1.00	.226	.126	.049	.043	.021	.117	−.159	**1.00**										
9	Temporal_Disp	1.00	.136	.084	.000	−.001	−.032	.046	−.101	.155	**1.00**									
10	Req_Instab	.893	.256	.243	.144	.073	.115	.115	−.052	.044	.057	**.823**								
11	Req_Div	.877	.315	250	.073	.097	.062	.120	−.175	.139	.099	.651	**.839**							
12	Tech_Div	1.00	.161	.130	.058	.128	.100	.087	−.272	.357	.100	.100	.189	**1.00**						
13	Task_inter	.827	.116	−.010	.316	.255	.294	.149	−.042	.086	.025	.273	.257	.075	**.784**					
14	Gender	1.00	.032	.029	−.059	−.036	−.008	−.049	.011	.007	−.004	.016	.043	−.038	−.019	**1.00**				
15	Care_for_Dep.	1.00	−.147	−.035	.015	−.021	−.050	004	.153	−.093	−.129	−.033	−.045	−.131	.034	.005	**1.00**			
16	Exp_DSD	1.00	−.020	−.128	.110	−.007	.022	.075	.140	.055	.000	−.012	−.027	−.002	.075	−.035	.020	**1.00**		
17	Role	1.00	.198	.081	.051	.020	.008	.104	−.206	.144	−.001	.059	.088	.167	.072	−.012	−.161	.024	**1.00**	
18	Country	1.00	.126	.129	−.062	−.045	−.100	−.010	−.234	.273	.018	−.018	.098	.175	−.027	−.017	−.205	−.204	.159	**1.00**

[a]Square roots of the AVEs are in the diagonal

Ylitalo (2011) for PLS. We used a variable that may be considered to be unrelated directly to WLC—namely, the industry to which the respondents' organization belonged. Using this as the marker variable, we tested our model, and the results indicated no change in the significance of our hypothesized paths.

Reference

U.S. vs. U.K. Employment Law: What's the Difference? (2012). Retrieved January 4, 2021, from https://ieglobal.vistra.com/blog/2012/2/us-vs-uk-employment-law-whats-difference.

Index

S. Sarker et al., *Navigating Work and Life Boundaries*,
https://doi.org/10.1007/978-3-030-72759-8

The manufacturer's authorised representative in the EU is Springer
Nature Customer Service Centre GmbH, Europaplatz 3, 69115 Heidelberg,
Germany. If you have any concerns regarding our products, please
contact ProductSafety@springernature.com

Printed and bound by CPI Group (UK) Ltd, Croydon, CR0 4YY

30/09/2026

02225457-0003